GUILD SOCIALISM RESTATED

GUILD SOCIALISM RESTATED

G. D. H. COLE

Volume 4

Routledge
Taylor & Francis Group
LONDON AND NEW YORK

First published 1920 by Routledge
4 Park Square, Milton Park, Abingdon, Oxon OX14 4RN
605 Third Avenue, New York, NY 10017

Routledge is an imprint of the Taylor & Francis Group, an informa business

First issued in paperback 2017

British Library Cataloguing in Publication Data
A catalogue record for this book is available from the British Library

ISBN 13: 978-0-415-56651-3 (Set)
ISBN 13: 978-0-415-59820-0 (Volume 4) (hbk)
ISBN 13: 978-0-8153-6972-1 (Volume 4) (pbk)

Publisher's Note
The publisher has gone to great lengths to ensure the quality of this reprint but
points out that some imperfections in the original copies may be apparent.

Disclaimer
The publisher has made every effort to trace copyright holders and would
welcome correspondence from those they have been unable to trace.

Guild Socialism
Restated

G.D.H. Cole

CONTENTS

GUILD SOCIALISM

CHAPTER I

THE DEMAND FOR FREEDOM

FOR any just appreciation of the social forces
at work in the world to-day, there is no fact
more essential to grasp than the broadening
and deepening demand of the organised
workers for the "control of industry." This
demand is made, not in one country or in one
form alone, but in nearly every country in
which the industrial system is strongly established, and in as many forms as there are
different national temperaments and traditions. Nor is the demand new; for it has
appeared, at least occasionally, throughout
the history of the Labour Movement, in the
"Owenite" Trade Unionism of the thirties
in Great Britain, among anarchists and communists on the Continent of Europe, and
among the early revolutionaries and reformers
of the United States. But its character at the
present time differs from any that it has pos-

sessed before, not only because it is more universal and has struck far deeper roots, but because it is now based firmly on the positive achievements of working-class organisation, and is no longer purely Utopian, but constructive and practical.

This book on Guild Socialism is an attempt to explain the real character of this demand, particularly as it appears amongst the English-speaking peoples, and at the same time to present the central ideas of Guild Socialism as above all an attempt to give theoretical and practical expression to the aspirations on which the demand is based. It is written in the belief that, until we devise and create forms of social organisation within which these aspirations can find reasonable satisfaction, there is neither hope of any " reconstruction " which will make our industrial system efficient nor prospect of health in the body social as a whole. Although, therefore, the way of approach and the main subject-matter of this book are industrial, its implications and conclusions will be found to extend over a considerably wider field than that of industry, and indeed to involve a theory of democratic representative government as a whole and constructive proposals governing the general lines of political as well as industrial reconstruction.

The Guild Socialist theory, while, like all other social theories, it makes certain fundamental assumptions concerning the objects of human association and men's life in Society, arises essentially out of the actual historical situation in which we are placed at the present time. The Guild Socialist believes what he believes, not so much as the result of a process of abstract reasoning, as because, if his fundamental assumptions are granted, the Guild Socialist solution of the social problem seems to him to spring simply and naturally out of the form in which that problem presents itself to-day. He claims, not to be imagining a Utopia in the clouds, but to be giving form and direction to certain quite definite tendencies which are now at work in Society, and to be anticipating the most natural developments of already existing institutions and social forces. He does not mind being called a " visionary " ; for he is quite convinced that his visions are eminently practical.

The best way, then, of understanding the Guild Socialist attitude is to see, first, what are the fundamental assumptions about Society which the Guildsman makes; secondly, how he visualises the situation with which the industrialised communities of Europe, America and Australasia are at present confronted ; and thirdly, what are the forces and institutions in whose development he believes that the solution of the problem principally lies. A correct appreciation of these points will clear the way for a constructive exposition of Guild Socialist proposals.

Guildsmen assume that the essential social values are human values, and that Society is to be regarded as a complex of associations held together by the wills of their members, whose well-being is its purpose. They assume further that it is not enough that the forms of government should have the passive or "implied" consent of the governed, but that the Society will be in health only if it is in the full sense democratic and self-governing, which implies not only that all the citizens should have a "right" to influence its policy if they so desire, but that the greatest possible opportunity should be afforded for every citizen actually to exercise this right. In other words, the Guild Socialist conception of democracy, which it assumes to be good, involves an active and not merely a passive citizenship on the part of the members. Moreover, and this is perhaps the most vital and significant assumption of all, it regards this democratic principle as applying, not only or mainly to some special sphere of social action known as "politics," but to any and every form of social action, and, in especial, to industrial and economic fully as much as to political affairs.

In calling these the fundamental assumptions of Guild Socialism, I do not mean to imply that they are altogether beyond the province of argument. They can indeed be sustained by arguments of obvious force; for it seems clear enough that only a community which is self-governing in this complete sense, over the whole length and breadth of its activities, can hope to call out what is best in its members, or to give them that maximum opportunity for personal and social self-expression which is requisite to real freedom. But such arguments as this, by which the assumptions stated above may be sustained and reinforced, really depend for their appeal upon the same considerations, and are, in the last resort, different ways of stating the same fundamental position. The essence of the Guild Socialist attitude lies in the belief that Society ought to be so organised as to afford the greatest possible opportunity for individual and collective self-expression to all its members, and that this involves and implies the extension of positive self-government through all its parts.

No one can reasonably maintain that Society is organised on such a principle to-day. We do, indeed, possess in theory a very large measure of democracy; but there are at least three sufficient reasons which make this theoretical democracy largely inoperative in practice. In the first place, even the theory of democracy to-day is still largely of the " consciousness of consent " type. It assigns to the ordinary citizen little more than a privilege—which is in practice mainly illusory—of choosing his rulers, and does not call upon him, or assign to him the opportunity, himself to rule.

Present-day practice has, indeed, pushed the theory of representative government to the length of substituting almost completely, even in theory, the representative for the represented. This is the essential meaning of the doctrine of the " sovereignty of Parliament." Secondly, such democracy as is recognised is conceived in a narrowly " political " sense, as applying to a quite peculiar sphere known as politics, and not in a broader and more comprehensive sense, as applying to all the acts which men do in association or conjunction. The result is that theoretical " democrats " totally ignore the effects of undemocratic organisation and convention in non-political spheres of social action, not only upon the lives which men lead in those spheres, but also in perverting and annihilating in practice the theoretical democracy of modern politics. They ignore the fact that vast inequalities of wealth and status, resulting in vast inequalities of education, power and control of environment, are necessarily fatal to any real democracy, whether in politics or in any other sphere. Thirdly, the theory of representative government is distorted not only by the substitution of the representative for the represented, but also as a consequence of the extended activity of political government falsifying the operation of the representative method. As long as the purposes of political government are comparatively few and limited, and the vast mass of social activities is either not regulated, or regulated by other means, such as the Mediaeval Gilds, it is perhaps possible for a body of men to choose one to represent them in relation to all the purposes with which a representative political body has to deal.[1] But, as the purposes covered by political government expand, and more and more of social life is brought under political regulation, the representation which may once, within its limitations, have been real, turns into misrepresentation, and the person elected for an indefinitely large number of disparate purposes ceases to have any real representative relation to those who elect him.

It appears to the Guild Socialists, as to all real Socialists, obviously futile to expect true democracy to exist in any Society which recognises vast inequalities of wealth, status and power among its members. Most obvious of all is it that, if, in the sphere of industry, one man is a master and the other a wage-slave, one enjoys riches and gives commands and the other has only an insecure subsistence and obeys orders, no amount of purely electoral machinery on a basis of " one man one vote " will make the two really equal socially or politically. For the economic power of the rich master, or of the richer financier who is

---

[1] Thus, government in Great Britain for some time after 1689 was a fairly adequate representation of the aristocracy, whom alone it set out to represent.

above even the master, will ring round the
wage-slave's electoral rights at every point. A
Press which can only be conducted with the
support of rich capitalists and advertisers, an
expensive machinery of elections, a régime in
the school which differs for rich and poor and
affords a training for power in the one case
and for subjection in the other, a régime in
industry which carries on the divergent lessons
of the schools—these and a hundred other
influences combine to make the real political
power of one rich man infinitely greater than
that of one who is poor. It is a natural and
legitimate conclusion that, if we want democracy, that is, if we want every man's voice
to count for as much as it is intrinsically worth,
irrespective of any extraneous consideration,
we must abolish class distinctions by doing
away with the huge inequalities of wealth and
economic power on which they really depend.

We are faced by the fact that, owing to the
preponderant influence of economic factors,
the present machinery of Society expresses
the point of view of the social class which still
continues to control its economic life. But at
the same time it is clear that the power of
this class is more and more challenged by its
rival—the working class—acting upon it
through the organisations which are becoming
more and more fully representative of all its
groups and sections. The principal social
phenomenon of our times is the rise of work-

ing-class organisation, first and foremost in its
Trade Union form, but also in the Co-operative
Movement and in other less important aspects.
This working-class organisation already represents a very great social power; but it is a
power unrecognised in the constitution.   It
may be said that it is no more extra-constitu-
tional than the even greater power of the huge
capitalist trusts and combines of which the
Federation of British Industries has assumed
the leadership; but the extra-constitutionality
of capitalist organisations hardly arises as a
practical question because they represent the
same class as now holds social and economic
authority in the community and political
authority in the State.   The workers, on the
other hand, as the dispossessed class both
economically and politically, have to employ
their industrial organisation as almost the sole
means at their disposal for making their will
felt, whatever the question at issue may be.
As they acquire a greater sense of their industrial strength, they seek to turn it to more
ambitious uses, and attempt to employ it as
an instrument of communal government.
This is essentially the meaning of " Direct
Action."

The form of economic organisation which
" Direct Action " challenges, regarded from
the upper end, is called " Capitalism."   Regarded from the lower end the same system
is properly called " Wage-Slavery."   It is so

called because it imposes, on the mass of those
who work under it, a quasi-servile status, and
because it does this by means of the wage
system.   The institution of wages is one by
which the employer or company is enabled to
buy labour, in the quantities in which it is
required as the raw material of profit, at a
market price not essentially differing from
the market price for ordinary commodities.
Labour may be bought cheap or dear, according to market conditions, or, if there is no
profit to be made out of it, it need not be
bought at all.   When the workman's labour
is bought, he receives a wage : when it is not
bought, he receives no wages.   In the latter
circumstances, the correct capitalist procedure
used to be either to leave him to starve or to
force him into the workhouse under the de-
terrent conditions of the " New Poor Law ";
but, this proving neither humane nor econom-
ical, the small provision which the better paid
workers succeeded in making for themselves
through their Trade Unions has in recent years
been supplemented by State and employers'
contributions in certain trades, and the workman has further been subjected to compulsory
deductions from his wages to provide against
periods of unemployment.   These doles, however, do not affect the fundamental fact that,
under the theory of Capitalism, the labourer
has no rights in industry.   He sells to the
capitalist, for what he can get, as much of his

labour-power as he can, and the whole of his claim upon what he produces is supposed to be liquidated by the payment of a wage. The whole value of his product, over and above his wages, is absorbed by others in the forms of rent, interest and profits.

This is, of course, a very inadequate summary; but it will suffice for our present purpose, which is only that of showing the breaches in the system which are already being made by the onslaughts of the growingly powerful working-class organisations. These achieve their results by rescuing the worker from isolation, and substituting for individual competitive sale by each worker of his labour-power rudimentary forms of collective bargaining, through which the Trade Unions prescribe, for all their members, minimum conditions under which the sale of labour-power is to take place. These conditions, as the power of the Unions grows, increase in number and stringency, and come to represent more and more actual interference by the workers with the way in which the industry is run.

The Trade Union, however, in all the regulations which it lays down, still always remains a body external to the actual conduct of industry. It cannot give actual orders as to the way in which factories are to be run : it can, broadly speaking, only impose prohibitions. This leads necessarily to the result that its action is to a great extent negative and restrictive, and thus operates in the same way as an externally imposed State law regulating industry, and possesses the same disadvantages. The further this external system of prohibitions is pushed, the greater difficulties it creates for the existing system. The employer complains, often with some justice, that he can no longer run his factory in his own way; but the Union on its side can only protect its members by hampering him, and has no positive power to run the factory in his stead. Smooth working is sometimes established in practice by a method of mutual give and take; but the whole system is essentially one of unstable equilibrium, and it seems clear, at any rate to the Guild Socialists, that there are only two possible alternatives. Either the power of the Unions to impose restrictions must be broken; or it must be transformed from a negative into a positive power, and, instead of having only the brake in their hands, the Trade Unions must assume control of the steering-wheel.[2]

This statement, purely in terms of contending economic powers, of the deadlock at which the present industrial system is arriving is essentially incomplete; for behind these powers are the wills that wield them. The deadlock exists, not simply or mainly because an equilibrium of powers is being reached, but also

[2] This ignores for the moment the supposed alternative of " joint control," which is discussed later, see p. 196.

because the psychological attitudes of the economic classes concerned in industry are undergoing, partly no doubt as a result of the changing balance of powers, a fundamental alteration. The capitalist system, or wage-system, as we have roughly outlined it above, was workable only as long as the various classes accepted willingly, or could be compelled to accept, their respective positions under it. In the early days of the factory system, and especially in the period of " Owenite " Trade Unionism and of the Chartist Movement, there was indeed a widespread revolt of the workers against a status and intolerable conditions which were then largely new ; but the power and organisation at their command were not then adequate to throw off the yoke, and they were compelled to accept a system in which they did not willingly acquiesce. The failure of their revolt, followed by a slight but real improvement of conditions led, to a great extent, to a mood of acquiescence ; and during the latter half of the nineteenth century the factory system was carried on with a considerable measure of resignation and even consent of the part of the workers, who still sought to improve their position under the system, but rarely, as they had done, to end it altogether. Towards the end of the century, after the growth of the modern Socialist Movement and the spread of organisation among new sections of workers, the mood of revolt began again to grow; but even down to the war period, despite the unrest of the years immediately preceding 1914, it had hardly reached dimensions sufficient seriously to alarm the governing classes, or to threaten the impending overthrow of the capitalist system.

The war, not so much by introducing new factors as by hastening immensely the operation of those which were already at work, completely altered the situation. Not in one, but in many countries, it brought the movement of revolt to a head, leading in some cases to actual revolution, but in far more to a state of tension which, without producing immediate revolution, threw the capitalist system largely out of gear. This occurred because everywhere the war brought to the organised working-class an immensely increased consciousness of their strength, and of the possibility of translating that strength into recognised and effective social power. It also largely discredited capitalism as a method of production and caused the State—the political machinery of Society—to assume more nakedly and obviously the shape of an instrument of class-domination. The Russian Revolution, moreover, however Bolshevism as a policy was regarded, produced everywhere a very powerful effect on the minds of the workers, and the knowledge of it, mingling in their consciousness with the other factors, created on their part a disposition far more ready for change. Add to this the fact that war breeds a disregard of minor consequences and a readiness for desperate remedies, and that it introduces a considerable dislocation into the working of the ordinary mechanism of Society, and into the factory most of all, and you have all the essential causes of the profound change which has come over the attitude of the working-class in all the industrialised countries.

This change of attitude was swift in producing a change in the actual industrial situation. Not only did it make the workers more ready to embark on disputes, both great and small, whether with the Government or with their employers : it also very greatly affected their everyday state of mind in the factory and at their work. Not only did they learn to strike more readily : they were visited by an increasing unwillingness to work for capitalist masters. The effect of this was seen at once not only in more constant factory bickerings, but also and far more in a rapid fall in individual output, which no application of " incentives to production," whether in the form of " payment by results " or of pamphlets and other exhortations to " produce more in the cause of industrial prosperity and national revival " availed to check. Thus, at the very moment when the external threat of the powerful working-class organisations to capitalist and the capitalist State began to look most threatening, the capitalist system began to find itself also undermined from within by the reluctance of the workers to serve it as well and faithfully as they had done in the past. Nor could this reluctance be effectively met by coercion; for the devils of hunger and fear, by which the workers had been driven back to the factories and compelled to produce in the days of the former revolts, have now, owing to the increased absolute power of the organised workers of to-day, lost most of their effect. Everywhere the workers are proceeding steadily with the undermining of the capitalist order of Society.

Guild Socialists, then, not merely envisage the present position as one that can only continue for a limited period and at the cost of progressive deterioration, and believe that they have rightly conceived of the best general form for the next stage of social development to assume : they also definitely pin their faith to an expansion, both in function and in membership, of the organisations which the workers have created for their own defence, and hold that the signs of this expansion are everywhere to be detected in the present tendencies of working-class policy. They see the clash between the old order and the new both as a struggle for power of rival social classes, possessing and dispossessed, and as a striving by the organised workers for the assumption of social functions which they feel themselves increasingly well able to perform in the common interest.   Moreover, the decreasing efficiency of capitalist industry and the lessened willingness of the workers to produce seem to Guildsmen the inevitable outcome of a situation in which the distribution of social status and authority has lost all correspondence with the real balance of economic competence.   Out of such a situation must come revolutionary   change,   with   or   without violence : the object of Guildsmen is to inform this coming revolution with a constructive spirit, and to devise for its furtherance a positive policy in harmony both with the aspirations of the common people and with the capacity of the organisation which the common people have made for their protection under capitalism.

Guild Socialism therefore appears largely as a theory of institutions and as a policy directed to the transformation of the social structure.   It is this, however, not because it believes that the life of men is comprehended in their social machinery, but because social machinery, as it is good or bad, harmonious or discordant with human desires and instincts, is the means either of furthering, or of thwarting, the expression of human personality.   If environment   does   not,   as   Robert   Owen thought, make character in an absolute sense, it does direct and divert character into divergent forms of expression.   Environment, in modern Societies at least, is very largely a matter of social mechanism. To get the mechanism right, and to adjust it as far as possible to the expression of men's social wills, is therefore the surest way, not only to the well-being of the body politic, but to the happiness and sense of well-directed achievement which chiefly constitute individual well-being. It is not because they idealise industrialism or social institutions that Guildsmen spend so much time in theorising and planning about them : it is because they see the best chance of human well-being in getting these aspects of life put firmly and properly into their right place.

CHAPTER II

THE BASIS OF DEMOCRACY

In the course of the last chapter the point was emphasised that for the constructive task of social reorganisation more is needed than a plan for the assumption of power by a social class, however equipped. There is also needed a positive plan of action for that class to pursue both in the course of and after its assumption of power. Guild Socialism claims to present the essential features of such a plan, based directly upon the workers' own organisations and assigning to them the leading rôle in the process of transformation.

As a necessary preliminary to the unfolding of this plan we have now to pursue the second line of criticism suggested in the preceding chapter, and to see wherein, even if we suppose the class character of existing Society to be eliminated, its social structure still fails to satisfy the conditions of reasonable human association and government which we have laid down as our fundamental assumptions. Of course, I do not deny that many of the features of present-day social structure which we shall have now to examine are indirectly the result of its class basis; but they are such as might, in theory at least, continue in existence after the abolition of social and economic classes, and their continuance has indeed hitherto been assumed to be desirable by many who call themselves Socialists.

Under the present system, the supreme legislative control of policy is supposed to reside in Parliament, and the supreme executive power in a Cabinet which is supposed to be a sort of committee of the parliamentary majority in the House of Commons. Theoretically, the competence of Parliament knows no limits, and it can pass laws dealing with any subject under the sun. Moreover, as the body politic becomes more diseased, the number and diversity of the laws which it passes and the subjects with which it deals steadily increase. It is true that at the same time the real power of Parliament wanes, and its functions are largely usurped by the Cabinet acting as the trustee of the great vested interests. This, however, does not concern us; for we are studying Parliament and Cabinet as they appear, with other institutions such as the standing army and the national police, in the form of the modern State.

The theory of State omni-competence has grown up gradually. Locke, a typical political philosopher of an earlier period, certainly regarded the State, not as " sovereign " in the sense now attaching to the term, but as strictly limited in function and capacity. There was a time, away back in the Middle Ages, when the State was only one of a number of social institutions and associations, all of which exercised, within their more or less clearly defined spheres of operation, a recognised social power and authority. During the period which followed the close of the Middle Ages, these other bodies were for the most part either swept away or reduced to impotence; but the effect of their disappearance was not, except to a limited extent for a time in the sixteenth and seventeenth centuries, the assumption of their powers by the State, but the passing of the social purposes which they had regulated outside the sphere of communal regulation altogether. Thus the ground was cleared for the unguided operation of the Industrial Revolution in the eighteenth and nineteenth centuries, and the vast structure of modern industrialism grew up without any attempt by Society, as an organised system, to direct it to the common advantage. This unregulated growth in its turn created the urgent need for intervention; and, all alternative forms of communal structure having been destroyed or submerged, it was the State which was called upon to intervene. Thus took place the vast extension of the sphere of State action, which, while it was partly protective in its origin, led to the confrontation of the pigmy man by a greater Leviathan, and produced a situation extremely inimical to personal liberty, of its real inroads upon which we are only now becoming fully sensible. As Mr. Belloc would say, it created the conditions in modern Society which are making for the Servile State.

The events of the last few years have opened the eyes of many to the real character of this development, and in particular have created a revolution in Socialist thought on the subject of the State. This is indeed a question on which Socialists have always been sharply divided; but the schools of Parliamentary Socialists, whether they have called themselves Marxian or not, have always, in opposition both to the industrial Socialists and to the catastrophic revolutionaries, been inclined to hold that Socialism would come about by the assumption by the people, or the workers, of the control of the State machine, that is by the conquest of parliamentary and political power. They have then conceived of the actual achievement of Socialism mainly by the use of this power for the expropriation of the rich, the socialisation of the means of production, and the re-organisation of industry under State ownership and under the full control of a Parliament dominated by Socialists. In fact, the only essential *structural* change to which they have looked forward, apart from the social and economic change involved in expropriation, is the completion of the present tendency towards State Sovereignty by the piling of fresh powers and duties on the great Leviathan.

If the fundamental assumptions on the basis of which we set out are right, this idea is certainly altogether wrong. For we assumed, not only that democracy ought to be fully applied to every sphere of organised social effort, but that democracy is only real when it is conceived in terms of function and purpose. In any large community, democracy necessarily involves representative government. Government, however, is not democratic if, as in most of the forms which pass for representative government to-day, it involves the substitution of the will of one man, the representative, for the wills of many, the represented. There are two respects in which the present form of parliamentary representation, as it exists in all " democratic " States to-day, flagrantly violates the fundamental principles of democracy. The first is that the elector retains practically no control over his representative, has only the power to change him at very infrequent intervals, and has in fact only a very limited range of choice.[1] The

---

[1] Nine times out of ten, he has only the choice of voting for the least futile or objectionable candidate, or of abstaining.

second is that the elector is called upon to
choose one man to represent him in relation
to every conceivable question that may come
before Parliament, whereas, if he is a rational
being, he always certainly agrees with one
man about one thing and with another about
another, or at any rate would do so as soon
as the economic basis of present class divisions
was removed.

The omnicompetent State, with its omnicompetent Parliament, is thus utterly unsuitable to any really democratic community, and
must be destroyed or painlessly extinguished
as it has destroyed or extinguished its rivals in
the sphere of communal organisation. Whatever the structure of the new Society may be,
the Guildsman is sure that it will have no place
for the survival of the *factotum* State of
to-day.

The essentials of democratic representation,
positively stated, are, first, that the represented shall have free choice of, constant contact with, and considerable control over, his
representative.[2] The second is that he should
be called upon, not to choose someone to
represent him as a man or as a citizen in all
the aspects of citizenship, but only to choose
someone to represent his point of view in relation to some particular purpose or group of
purposes, in other words, some particular

---

[2] I am not suggesting that the representative should be reduced to
the status of a delegate. But on this see later, p. 133ff.

function. All true and democratic representation is therefore *functional* representation.

The structure of any democratic Society must be in harmony with these essential principles. Where it employs the representative method, this must be always in relation to some definite function. It follows that there must be, in the Society, as many separately elected groups of representatives as there are distinct essential groups of functions to be performed. Smith cannot represent Brown, Jones and Robinson as human beings; for a human being, as an individual, is fundamentally incapable of being represented. He can only represent the common point of view which Brown, Jones and Robinson hold in relation to some definite social purpose, or group of connected purposes. Brown, Jones and Robinson must therefore have, not one vote each, but as many different functional votes as there are different questions calling for associative action in which they are interested.

It should be noted that the argument, up to the point to which we have at present carried it, does not suggest or prescribe any particular type of constituency or arrangement of the franchise. It does not lay down that men should vote by geographical, or that they should vote by occupational, constituencies, or that they should do both. All that we have yet established is that man should have as

3

many distinct, and separately exercised, votes,
as he has distinct social purposes or interests.
But the democratic principle applies, not only
to the whole body of citizens in a community
in relation to each set of purposes which they
have in common, but also and equally to each
group of citizens who act in co-operation for
the performance of any social function or who
possess a common social interest. There are
indeed two distinct kinds of bond which may
link together in association members of the
same community, and each of these bonds may
exist either between all or between some of
the members. The first bond is that of common vocation, the performance in common of
some form of social service, whether of an
economic character or not : the second bond
is that of common interest, the receiving,
using or consuming of such services. In the
working-class world to-day, Trade Unionism
is the outstanding example of the former type,
and Co-operation of the latter.

In a democratic community, it is essential
that the principle of self-government should
apply to the affairs of every one of the associations arising out of either of these forms
of common purpose. It is, from this point
of view, immaterial whether a particular association includes all, or only some, of the
whole body of citizens, provided that it adequately represents those who possess the common purpose which it exists to fulfil. Thus,

the form of representative government or administration required for each particular service or interest will be that which most adequately represents the persons concerned in it.

But, it will be said, surely to a great extent everything is everybody's concern. It is certainly not the exclusive concern of the coal miners, or of the workers in any other particular industry, how their service is conducted; for everybody, including every other industry, is concerned as a consumer of coal. Nor is it by any means the exclusive concern of the teachers what the educational system is, or how it is administered; for the whole people is concerned in education as the greatest civic service. On the other hand, the coal industry clearly concerns the miner, and education concerns the teacher, in a way different from that in which they concern the rest of the people; for, whereas for the latter coal is only one among a number of commodities, and education one among several civic services, to the miner or the teacher his own calling is the most important single concern in social life.[3]

This distinction really brings us to the heart of our problem, and to the great practical difference between Guild Socialism and other schools of Socialist opinion. For the Guilds-

3 Of course, I am not here attempting to estimate its importance in relation to his personal concerns, or to the family, which fall outside the scope of social organisation, except among modern Prussians and eugenists.

man maintains that in a right apprehension of
this distinction, and in the framing of social
arrangements which recognise and make full
provision for it, lies the key to the whole
question at issue. It is absurd to deny the
common interest which all the members of the
community have, as consumers and users, in
the vital industries, or as sharers of a common
culture and code in such a service as education;
but it is no less futile to deny the special, and
even more intense, concern which the miners
have in the organisation of their industry, or
the teachers in the conduct of the educational
system.

Nevertheless, there are schools of Socialist,
or quasi-Socialist thought, which take their
stand upon each of these impossible denials.
The Collectivist, or State Socialist, who regards the State as representing the consumer,
and the purely "Co-operative" idealist, who
sees in Co-operation a far better consumers'
champion, are alike in refusing to recognise
the claim of the producer, or service renderer,
to self-government in his calling. The pure
"Syndicalist," or the pure "Industrial
Unionist," on the other hand, denies, or at
least used to deny, the need of any special
representation of the consumers' standpoint,
and presses for an organisation of Society
based wholly on production or the rendering
of service.

It is true that, in their extreme forms, both

these antagonistic views are dying out, the pressure of each upon the other, and of Guild Socialism upon both, having compelled modification in both cases. But the ordinary State Socialist or Co-operative idealist to-day still stresses mainly the claim of the consumer and allows only a very subordinate and "discreetly regulated" freedom to the producer; while there are still many who lay nearly all the emphasis upon the producer, and give only a very grudging and half-hearted assent to the claims of the consumer for self-determination.

It has been the work of Guild Socialism to hold the balance between these two schools of thought, not by splitting the difference, but by pointing out that the solution lies in a clear distinction of function and sphere of activity. The phrase "control of industry"[4] is in fact loosely used to include the claims of both producers and consumers; but it has, in the two uses, really to a great extent different meanings, and, still more, different associations. When the "Syndicalist" or the Guild Socialist speaks of the need for control by the producers, or when a Trade Union itself demands control, the reference is mainly to the internal conditions of the industry, to the way in which the factory or place of work is

[4] For the rest of this chapter I shall speak only in terms of industry, and not of services such as education, not because I think that one phraseology or treatment will cover both, but because I am reserving the "civic services" for separate discussion. See Chapter VI.

managed, the administrators appointed, the conditions determined, and, above all, to the amount of freedom *at his work* which the worker by hand or brain enjoys. When, on the other hand, a State Socialist or a Co-operator speaks of the need for "consumers' control," he is thinking mainly of the quantity and quality of the goods supplied, of the excellence of the distribution, of the price of sale—in short, of a set of considerations which, while they are intimately bound up with those which chiefly concern the producer, are still in essence distinct, and have to do far less with the internal conduct of the industry than with its external relations. They are, so to speak, its "foreign politics" as viewed by the foreigners.

Naturally, if these vital distinctions are not made, each of the claimants to "control of industry" is inclined to claim the whole, or at best to relegate the other to a quite subordinate position. Moreover, even when the distinction is clearly stated, there is a strong temptation for those who belong to either movement to claim too much for their own. The Guild Socialist endeavours to hold the scales fairly, and to decide, as far as the matter can be decided except in practice, what are the fair claims on each side.

In doing this, the Guildsman has not to face any problem of arbitrating between divergent interests. In a democratic Society, the whole body of consumers and the whole body of producers are practically the same people, only ranged in the two cases in different formations. There can be no real divergence of interests between them. It is a problem not, as in present-day Society, of economic warfare, but of reasonable democratic organisation on a functional basis.

The Guild Socialist contends, then, that the internal management and control of each industry or service must be placed, as a trust on behalf of the community, in the hands of the workers engaged in it; but he holds no less strongly that full provision must be made for the representation and safeguarding of the consumers' point of view in relation to each service. Similarly, he contends that general questions of industrial administration extending to all industries should, where they mainly concern the whole body of producers, be entrusted to an organisation representing all the producers; but he holds equally that the general point of view of all types of consumers must be fully represented and safeguarded in relation to industry as a whole. The mere detailed working out of this principle will occupy a considerable part of this book : and for the present it must be left in the shape of a generalisation. I claim, however, that, so far as it goes, it satisfies the conditions of democracy in a way which neither State Socialism, nor Co-operativism, nor Syndicalism, nor any alternative proposal hitherto brought forward is able to parallel.

This, however, may be dismissed by " practically-minded " people as a purely theoretical disquisition, and it is therefore advisable to state the case in a more practical way, by relating it closely to what was said in the last chapter concerning the changing psychology of the workers. Let us therefore ask ourselves whether, if all industry passed under the management of a " State," however democratic, or of a Co-operative Movement, however enlightened, the workers engaged in its various branches would have the sense of being free and self-governing in relation to their work. It is true that they would be voters in the democratic State, or members of the Co-operative Society, and would therefore, in a sense, be ultimately part-controllers in some degree of their conditions; but would they regard this as freedom, when, although their concern in the internal arrangements of their industry was far closer than that of others, they had at most only the same voice with others in determining them. Obviously, the answer is that they neither would, nor could be expected to, take any such view; for, by the time their share in determining conditions had gone its roundabout course through the consumers' organisation, it would have ceased to be recognisable as even the most indirect sort of freedom. Men will never recognise or regard as self-government in any association a system which does not give to them directly as a group the right of framing their common rules to govern their internal affairs, and of choosing, by their own decisions, those who are to hold office and authority in their midst.

This being so, no solution of the problem of industrial government is really a solution at all unless it places the rights and responsibilities of the internal conduct of industry directly upon the organised bodies of producers. On no other condition will men who have risen to a sense of social capacity and power consent to serve or to give of their best. Any other attempted solution will therefore break down before the unwillingness of the workers to produce, and will afford no way of escape from the *impasse* to which we have already been brought by the denial under capitalism of the human rights of Labour. It is our business, then, to accept unreservedly this claim of the producer, and at the same time to reconcile it with the consumer's claim that his voice shall also count. We shall see that there is nothing impossible or even difficult in this reconciliation.

Note.—In this chapter I have not challenged the correctness of the State Socialist claim that the State "represents the consumer." I may say, however, here that I do not accept this contention, and therefore do not equate State with Co-operative management of industry. As, however, State Socialists and Co-operativists use the same arguments in favour of consumers' management, the difference between them does not arise in connection with this chapter. See later, page 84, where the point is dealt with more fully.

CHAPTER III

A GUILD IN BEING

THE name " Guild " is taken from the Middle Ages.   Throughout the mediæval period the predominant form of industrial organisation throughout the civilisation of Christendom was the Gild or Guild, an association of independent producers or merchants for the regulation of production or sale.   The mediæval Gild was not indeed confined to industry : it was the common form of popular association in the mediæval town.   There were Gilds for social and charitable, and for educational, as well as for industrial purposes ; and every Gild, whatever its specific function, had a strong religious basis and an essentially religious form. This is not the place to enter into a discussion of the rise, organisation and decline of the mediæval system ; but it is necessary to show, both what are the fundamental differences between mediæval Gilds and modern Guilds,[1] and what is the essential unity of idea between them.

[1] I have adopted the more correct " Gild " in speaking of the industrial organisation of the Middle Ages, while retaining the more familiar " Guild " to denote the modern theory.

42

The mediæval Gild was essentially local, and the Gilds in a single town formed a separate system. This applies less to the merchant than to the craft bodies, but it is true as a generalisation, and especially true of the British Gilds. This fact, which corresponds to the comparative localisation of markets owing to the scanty facilities for transit, of course largely accounts for the break-up of the Gilds at the close of the Middle Ages. The mediæval Gild again was an association of independent producers, each of whom worked on his own with a small number of journeymen and apprentices. It was an organisation based on small-scale handicraft production, and it broke down before the accumulation of wealth which made large-scale enterprise possible. The Gild was a regulative rather than a directly controlling or managing body. It did not itself manage the industry, though it sometimes acted as a purchasing agent for materials : it left actual management in the hands of its members, the master-craftsmen ; but it laid down elaborate regulations governing the actions and professional code of the members. These regulations, which are the essence of the mediæval Gild system, had as their basis the double object of maintaining both the liberties and rights of the craft and its tradition of good workmanship and faithful communal service, as expressed in the " Just Price." They declared war on shoddy work, on extortion and usury, and on unregulated

production.   They afforded to their members
a considerable security, and an assured communal status.   They held, in mediæval Society,
a recognised position as economic organs of the
body social, possessing a tradition of free service, and, on the strength of that tradition,
filling an honourable place in the public life of
the mediæval City.

I am far from contending that the Gilds were
perfect, or that they always, even in their best
days, lived up to the full demands of their principles.   Certainly, in the days of their decline,
when they were fighting a losing battle in a
hostile environment, they departed very far
from their tradition.   But we are concerned
less with their actual achievement—which was,
for a period of centuries, very great indeed—
than with the spirit which animated them, and
the principles upon which their power was
based.   We want to see what in these principles is of value to us in confronting the
problems of our own time, and, if their spirit
is one that we would gladly recapture, what
lessons we can learn from them concerning the
foundation on which this spirit rested.   For a
fundamental difference between mediæval industry and industry to-day is that the former
was imbued through and through with the spirit
of free communal service, whereas this motive
is almost wholly lacking in modern industrialism, and the attempt to replace it by the
motives of greed on one side and fear on the

other is manifestly breaking down. It is undoubtedly the case that, though there were sharp practices and profiteering in the Middle Ages, the Gildsman or the Gild that committed or sanctioned them did so in flat violation of moral principles which he or it had explicitly accepted as the basis of the industrial order, whereas to-day moral principles are regarded almost as intruders in the industrial sphere, and many forms of sharp practice and profiteering rank as the highest manifestations of commercial sagacity. In the Middle Ages, there were industrial sinners, but they were conscious of sin; for commercial morality and communal morality were the same. To-day, commercial morality has made a code of its own, and most of its clauses are flat denials of the principles of communal morality. In the Middle Ages, the motives to which the industrial system made its appeal were motives of free communal service: to-day, they are motives of greed and fear.

Clearly, we cannot seek to restore the mediæval—that is, the communal—spirit in industry by restoring the material conditions of the Middle Ages. We cannot go back to " town economy," a general régime of handicraft and master-craftsmanship, tiny-scale production. We can neither pull up our railways, fill in our mines, and dismantle our factories, nor conduct our large-scale enterprises under a system developed to fit the needs of a local market and a narrowly-restricted production. If the mediæval system has lessons for us, they are not parrot-lessons of slavish imitation, but lessons of the spirit, by which we may learn how to build up, on the basis of large-scale production and the world-market, a system of industrial organisation that appeals to the finest human motives and is capable of developing the tradition of free communal service.   I fully believe that, when we have established these free conditions, there will come, from producer and consumer alike, a widespread demand for goods of finer quality than the shoddy which we turn out in such quantity to-day, and that this will bring about a new standard of craftsmanship and a return, over a considerable sphere, to small-scale production. But this, if it comes, will come only as the deliberate choice of free men in a free Society. Our present problem is, taking the conditions of production substantially as we find them, to reintroduce into industry the communal spirit, by re-fashioning industrialism in such a way as to set the communal motives free to operate.

The element of identity between the mediæval Gilds and the National Guilds proposed by the Guild Socialists to-day is thus far more of spirit than of organisation. A National Guild would be an association of all the workers by hand and brain concerned in the carrying on of a particular industry or service, and its function would be actually to carry on that industry or service on behalf of the whole community. Thus, the Railway Guild would include all the workers of every type—from general managers and technicians to porters and engine cleaners required for the conduct of the railways as a public service. This association would be entrusted by the community with the duty and responsibility of administering the railways efficiently for the public benefit, and would be left itself to make the internal arrangements for the running of trains and to choose its own officers, administrators, and methods of organisation.

I do not pretend to know or prophesy exactly how many Guilds there would be, or what would be the lines of demarcation between them. For example, railways and road transport might be organised by separate Guilds, or by a single Guild with internal sub-divisions. So might engineering and ship-building, and a host of other closely-related industries. This is a matter, not of principle, but of convenience ; for there is no reason why the various Guilds should be of anything like uniform size. The general basis of the proposed Guild organisation is clear enough : it is industrial, and each National Guild will represent a distinct and coherent service or group of services.

It must not, however, be imagined that Guildsmen are advocating a highly centralised system, in which the whole of each industry will be placed under a rigid central control. The degree of centralisation will largely depend on the character of the service. Thus, the railway industry obviously demands a much higher degree of centralisation than the building industry, which serves mainly a local market. But, apart from this, Guildsmen are keen advocates of the greatest possible extension of local initiative and of autonomy for the small group, in which they see the best chance of keeping the whole organisation keen, fresh and adaptable, and of avoiding the tendency to rigidity and conservatism in the wrong things, so characteristic of large-scale organisation, and especially of trusts and combines under capitalism to-day. The National Guilds would be, indeed, for the most part co-ordinating rather than directly controlling bodies, and would be concerned more with the adjustment of supply and demand than with the direct control or management of their several industries. This will appear more plainly when we have studied the internal organisation of the Guilds.

The members of the Guild will be scattered over the country, in accordance with the local distribution of their particular industry, and will be at work in the various factories, mines, or other productive units belonging to their form of service. The factory, or place of work, will be the natural unit of Guild life. It will be, to a great extent, internally self-governing, and it will be the unit and basis of the wider local and national government of the Guild. The freedom of the particular factory as a unit is of fundamental importance, because the object of the whole Guild system is to call out the spirit of free service by establishing really democratic conditions in industry.   This democracy, if it is to be real, must come home to, and be exercisable directly by, every individual member of the Guild.   He must feel that he is enjoying real self-government and freedom *at his work;* or he will not work well and under the impulse of the communal spirit. Moreover, the essential basis of the Guild being associative service, the spirit of association must be given free play in the sphere in which it is best able to find expression.   This is manifestly the factory, in which men have the habit and tradition of working together.   The factory is the natural and fundamental unit of industrial democracy.   This involves, not only that the factory must be free, as far as possible, to manage its own affairs, but also that the democratic unit of the factory must be made the basis of the larger democracy of the Guild, and that the larger organs of Guild administration and government must be based largely on the principle of factory[2] representation.   This

[2] It should be understood throughout that, when I speak thus of the " factory," I mean to include under it also the mine, the shipyard, the dock, the station, and every corresponding place which is a natural centre of production or service.   Every industry has some more or less close equivalent for the factory.

raises, of course, important financial considerations, which will be dealt with in their place, when we discuss the financial basis of the Guild Socialist community.

Before, however, we attempt to consider in detail how either a Guild factory or the larger administrative machinery of a Guild would be organised, it is necessary to discuss certain general questions which affect the whole character of the organisation. I have spoken of the Guilds as examples of " industrial democracy " and " democratic association," and we must understand clearly wherein this Guild democracy consists, and especially how it bears on the relations between the different classes of workers included in a single Guild. For since a Guild includes *all* the workers by hand and brain engaged in a common service, it is clear that there will be among its members very wide divergences of function, of technical skill, and of administrative authority. Neither the Guild as a whole nor the Guild factory can determine all issues by the expedient of the mass vote, nor can Guild democracy mean that, on all questions, each member is to count as one and none as more than one. A mass vote on a matter of technique understood only by a few experts would be a manifest absurdity, and, even if the element of technique is left out of account, a factory administered by constant mass votes would be neither efficient nor at all a pleasant place to work in. There will be in

the Guilds technicians occupying special positions by virtue of their knowledge, and there
will be administrators possessing special
authority by virtue both of skill and ability and
of personal qualifications.   What are to be the
methods of choosing these officers and administrators within the Guild, and what are to be
their powers and relation to the other members
when they have been chosen?

The question of " leadership," " discipline,"
" authority " in their relation to the democratic principle is, of course, as old as the
earliest discussions of democracy itself.   The
difference between democracy and autocracy
is not that the latter recognises leadership and
the former does not, but that in democracy the
leader stands in an essentially different relation
to those whom he leads, and, instead of substituting his will for theirs, aims at carrying
out, not their " real will " as interpreted by
him,[3] but their actual will as understood by
themselves.   In short, the democratic leader
leads by influence and co-operation and not by
the forcible imposition of his will.   Leading in
this way, he may and should have not less, but
far more, " authority " than the autocrat,
because he is carrying with him the wills of
those whom he leads.   A democratic Guild
will have leaders, discipline and authority in a
fuller and more real sense than these can exist
under the industrial autocracy of capitalism.

---

[3] As in Bonapartist pseudo-democracies.

How, then, will these Guild leaders be chosen? That it will be by the Guild itself goes without saying ; for their imposition upon it from without would at once and utterly destroy its democratic character. But this does not mean that every type of leader must be chosen by a mass ballot of the whole Guild.

Let us begin our answer by removing from the discussion the man who is chosen, mainly or exclusively because he possesses a particular technical qualification, for the performance of a function which is essentially technical. He is not really a leader, but a consultant or adviser, and the matter of choosing him is an expert question which does not raise the democratic issue. It is for the leaders in the real sense—the men who, while they may require special expert skill or technical knowledge, are not chosen for these alone, but mainly for personal character or ability—the men whose work is mainly that of directing the work of others, of moving the energies of a group of men towards an accepted end, of expressing the corporate solidarity and co-operative spirit of the group—that we are here concerned to find the right principle of choice. To me it seems clear that, for any function which demands thus essentially the co-operations of wills, the only right principle is that the person who is to perform it should be chosen by those in co-operation with whom it is to be exercised. That is to say, the governing principle in the choice of

Guild leaders will be election " from below,"
by those whom the leaders will have to lead.

This principle, however, is fully compatible
with certain necessary safeguards.   Whenever
a post requires, in addition to personal fitness
for leadership, of which those who are to be led
are the best judges, definite qualifications of
skill or technique, the possession of these
qualifications can be made a condition of
eligibility for the position.   A shipowner
to-day can only appoint as captain of his ship
a man who holds a master's certificate.   The
seamen of the future Guild will only be able to
choose as their captain a man who is similarly
equipped.   And such certificates of technical
qualification will be issued, as they are in some
cases to-day, by bodies predominantly representative of those already qualified, but with
safeguards against the adoption by such bodies
of an unduly exclusive attitude.

Again, there is no need to lay it down as a
rigid principle that the leader must, in every
case, be chosen by the actual group of workers
whom he is to lead, and that no other worker
of the same calling is to play any part in the
choice.   I believe, indeed, that, in nine cases
out of ten at least, the right way is for the
actual group that needs a leader to choose him,
and that, with the full establishment of industrial democracy, this method would become
practically universal ; but there is no need to
make it a rigid rule, provided that in every case

the choice is made by men who are subject to similar leadership within the same calling and over a reasonably small area. Thus, the managers of a number of building jobs in the same district might conceivably be best appointed by the building workers of the district as a whole, rather than by the workers on each particular job; but this is an exception, due to the shifting character of building operations. As a general practice, the men on the job should choose their leaders for the job.

This applies with the greatest force of all in the smallest area over which industrial leadership is normally exercised. It is indispensable to industrial democracy that the foremen, the first grade of industrial supervisors, should be chosen directly by the particular body of men with whom they are to work; for, unless they are so chosen, the spirit of co-operation will not be set flowing at its source, and the whole organisation will be deprived of its democratic impulse. Within the factory, direct election by the individual workers concerned will probably be the best way of choosing nearly all the leaders; but, when units of organisation larger than the factory are reached, I do not suggest that direct election by the whole body of workers is any longer the best or the most democratic course. Election by delegates representing the whole body may often be better and more democratic. This, however, raises the whole question of direct *versus* indirect election, with which I shall have to deal later in connection with a very much wider problem.

This discussion of the methods of choosing leaders under a democratic industrial system may seem to be somewhat dull and detailed; but it is one of the fundamental problems of Guild Socialism. For the most frequent argument urged against industrial democracy is that it is incompatible with workshop discipline and productive efficiency, and recent utterances of the Russian Bolshevik leaders seem to indicate that they have come round, temporarily at least, to this view. Let us admit immediately that the institution suddenly to-day of a complete system of democratic choice of leaders such as I have outlined would be attended by enormous difficulties. The workers have no experience of industrial democracy : they have been accustomed to regard those who hold authority in capitalist industry as their natural enemies; and they could not, in a moment, revise the habits of a lifetime, or become fully imbued, in a day or a year, with the new conception of leadership as a co-operation of wills. The new system will have to make its way gradually, and it will not be perfectly and securely established until it too has become an instinct and a tradition. We have, however, in the long run, no alternative to trying it; for the old idea of leadership by the imposition of will is breaking down with the old industrial system.

We must not, then, in estimating the merits and possibilities of democratic leadership, concentrate our attention too much on the difficulties which would attend its instantaneous introduction : we must try to imagine it as it would be after a period of experience, when the workers were getting used to it, and the purely initial difficulties had been overcome. What, under these conditions, would be the new relation between the leader and those whom he would have to lead?

In a certain sense, he would clearly be less powerful. He could not, in a democratic Guild association, have the uncontrolled power of the " sack," the right to send a man to privation and possibly worse without appeal. For the Guild members would insist that a man threatened with dismissal should be tried by his peers, and every Guildsman would surely have behind him a considerable measure of economic security. Nor would he be able to ignore public opinion in the factory or in the Guild as a whole as a capitalistic manager can ignore it. But to set against these losses—if they were to be so regarded—he would have far more than countervailing gains. He would have a good prospect, if he used ordinary commonsense, of having the public opinion of the factory decisively on his side in his attempt to make things go well and smoothly : he would be able to look for a keen desire on the part of the workers to co-operate with him in producing the best results, and, at the worst, there could be between him and them no such barrier as is presented by the fact that the manager in a factory to-day holds his position as the nominee of a capitalist employer.

I strongly suspect that the managers in such a Guild factory would have no cause to complain of lack of power. If they wanted authority, they would find ample scope for it; but I believe most of them would soon cease to think of their positions mainly in terms of power, and would come to think of them instead mainly in terms of function. Only under the free conditions of democratic industry would the leader find real scope for leadership, and he would find it in a way that would enable him to concentrate all his faculties on the development of his factory as a communal service, instead of being, as now, constantly thwarted and restrained by considerations of shareholders' profit. There is no class of "industrious persons," as the Chartists would have said, to whom the Guild idea ought to have a stronger appeal than to the managers and technicians of industry; for it alone offers them full opportunities to use their ability in co-operation with their fellow-workers and for the service of their fellow-men.

A Guild factory, then, would be a natural centre of self-government, no longer, like the

factories of to-day, a mere prison of boredom
and useless toil, but a centre of free service and
associative enterprise. There would, of course,
be dull and unpleasant work still to be done in
the world; but even this would be immeasur-
ably lightened if it were done under free conditions and if the right motives were enlisted on
its side.[4]

In this factory there would doubtless be
workshop committees, meetings, debates, voting, and all the phenomena of democratic
organisation; but, though these are essential,
they are not so much of the quintessence of the
new thing as the co-operative spirit which they
exist to safeguard. Given free choice of leaders
and free criticism of them when chosen, a good
deal of the mere machinery of democracy might
remain normally in the background.

But there is one further point on which we
must touch in order to make our picture of the
leader's position complete. What security of
tenure would he have, and how could he be
removed if he failed to give satisfaction? The
workers who chose their manager need not have
an unrestricted right to recall him at any
moment. Before he could be deposed, he
should have the right to appeal to his peers—
his fellow-managers; and, if they held him in

---

[4] Moreover, how much of the world's really dull or unpleasant work
could we do away with if we really gave our minds to that instead of
to profit-mongering! Machinery would make short work of much; and
much we could simply do without.

the right, but the workers still desired his dismissal, the case should go for judgment to a higher tribunal of the Guild. But even so I think that after a certain lapse of time the workers under him should have the right to remove him; for a sustained desire to do so would prove incompatibility of temperament, which would unfit him for the co-operative task of democratic leadership in that particular factory. He might go through no fault of his own; but in that case he would be likely soon to find an opening elsewhere.

This factory of ours is, then, to the fullest extent consistent with the character of its service, a self-governing unit, managing its own productive operations, and free to experiment to the heart's content in new methods, to develop new styles and products, and to adapt itself to the peculiarities of a local or individual market. This autonomy of the factory is the safeguard of Guild Socialism against the dead level of mediocrity, the more than adequate substitute for the variety which the competitive motive was once supposed to stimulate, the guarantee of liveliness, and of individual work and workmanship.

With the factory thus largely conducting its own concerns, the duties of the larger Guild organisations would be mainly those of co-ordination, of regulation, and of representing the Guild in its external relations. They would, where it was necessary, co-ordinate the production of various factories, so as to make supply coincide with demand.   They would probably act largely as suppliers of raw materials and as marketers of such finished products as were not disposed of directly from the factory.   They would lay down general regulations, local or national, governing the methods of organisation and production within the Guild, they would organise research, and they would act on behalf of the Guild in its relations both with other Guilds, and with other forms of organisation, such as consumers' bodies, within the community, or with bodies abroad.

This larger Guild organisation, as we have seen, while it need not conform in all cases to any particular structure, must be based directly on the various factories included in the Guild. That is to say, the district Guild Committee must represent the various factories belonging to the Guild in the district, and probably also in most cases must include representatives of the various classes of workers, by hand or brain, included in the Guild.   The national Committee must similarly represent districts and classes of workers, in order that every distinct point of view, whether of a district or of a section, may have the fullest possible chance of being stated and considered by a representative body.   To the choice of the district and national officers of the Guild much the same arguments apply as to that of other leaders, save that, as we saw, over the larger areas indirect may often afford a more truly democratic result than direct election.

The essential thing about this larger organisation is that its functions should be kept down to the minimum possible for each industry. For it is in the larger organisation and in the assumption by it of too much centralised power that the danger of a new form of bureaucracy resulting in the ossification of the Guild may be found.   A small central and district organisation, keeping within a narrow interpretation of the functions assigned to it, may be an extraordinarily valuable influence in stimulating a sluggish factory ; but a large central machine will inevitably at the same time aim at concentrating power in its own hands and tend to reduce the exercise of this power to a matter of routine.   If the Guilds are to revive craftsmanship and pleasure in work well done ; if they are to produce quality as well as quantity, and to be ever keen to devise new methods and utilise every fresh discovery of science without loss of tradition ; if they are to breed free men capable of being good citizens both in industry and in every aspect of communal life ; if they are to keep alive the motive of free service— they must at all costs shun centralisation.   Fortunately, there is little doubt that they will do so ; for men freed from the double centralised autocracy of capitalist trust and capitalist State are not likely to be anxious to make for themselves a new industrial Leviathan.   They will rate their freedom high ; and highest they will rate that which is nearest to them and most affects their daily life—the freedom of the factory, of the place in which their common service to the community is done.

CHAPTER IV

THE GUILD SYSTEM IN INDUSTRY

In the last chapter, I attempted to present a picture of the working of a Guild as a democratic industrial association. We have now to study the working of the Guilds as an industrial system, their relations one with another, and their extension over the field of industry and commerce. And here the first question that faces us is whether the Guild method of organisation is suitable to all industries, or whether, in certain cases, other forms of organisation will have to be devised to work side by side, and in harmony, with the Guilds.

This is by no means a simple question to answer; for it requires a good deal of explanation in order to make its meaning plain. It is manifest that, in most of its details, the National Guild proposal has been worked out mainly in relation to the great large-scale industries and services which dominate modern economic life. On the other hand, there is certainly nothing in the fact either that an industry is small, or that it follows methods of small-scale production, to make it unsuitable for Guild organisation.   Indeed, in many respects those small-scale industries in which the element of craftsmanship most exists will find it easiest to understand and adopt the Guild form and the Guild spirit.   It is, however, the case that the field of industry includes, in addition to certain forms of production and service which are clearly distinct and capable of national co-ordination, others which are more scattered and difficult to attach to any national combination.   This applies above all to factories manufacturing a highly individual form of product, or catering for a quite special taste.

The National Guild form of organisation should be loose and elastic enough to admit into a single Guild many varieties of factory, and the greater part of these " individual " factories would attach themselves to a National Guild.   But I can see no objection to—rather every advantage in—factories which do not naturally form such an attachment remaining independent.   With the National Guild form of organisation predominant in industrial Society, such factories would, of course, have to conform to the vital Guild conditions, and they would, in most cases, naturally assume themselves a Guild form and reproduce almost exactly the structure, and perhaps even more perfectly express the spirit, of the Guild system.   Just as factory autonomy is vital in order to keep the Guild system alive and vigorous, the existence of varying democratic types -of factories in independence of the National Guilds may also be a means of valuable experiment and fruitful initiative of individual minds.   In insistently refusing to carry their theory to its last " logical " conclusion, the Guildsmen are true to their love of freedom and varied social enterprise.

Moreover, I, at any rate, if I can see the Guild system firmly established in the main industries, feel no anxiety that the forms of organisation which survive or are created in the rest of industry will be out of harmony with the Guild idea.   Above all, I would let alone, and leave with the greatest possible freedom of development, the small independent producer or renderer of service, leaving it to the future to determine how far the services in which he is engaged are naturally led to adopt definitely Guild forms, or only to bring their organisation into harmony with essential Guild principles. An attack on the independent producer in the interests of large-scale organisation would be a fatal step for the Guild system, and, providing that his operations can be purged of the capitalist taint and the opportunity of exploiting labour removed, it is much best to " let well alone."   This applies not only to small workshops and craftsmen, but also to many

5

professions, and, in special ways which require further detailed discussion, to some kinds of tradesmen in the business of distribution and to the farmers in agriculture.

It follows that there is no need in all cases to claim for each National Guild a monopoly of its own form of production. There is need for it to take over and guildise all capitalist concerns, and all concerns that cannot adapt themselves to essential Guild principles and to the democratic spirit; but actual monopoly, while it may be necessary in some instances, and may arise naturally in such cases as mines and railways, is at best always a necessary evil, even for a Guild. The " monopoly of Labour " is a necessary instrument for fighting capitalism; but it would not be wise to build the new order in the spirit of monopoly. I do not mean that I contemplate the existence of two National Guilds administering the same kind of service; but there might well be in some cases several regional or local Guilds, and in others factories not connected with the National Guild of their industry or service.

Apart from such exceptions, however, which would extend in all over only a small part of the field of industry, the Guild system is put forward as a plan of general industrial application. Under it all the great industries of production, transport and distribution are capable of being conducted, in respect both of their properly industrial and of their commercial aspects.   The financial system, and especially industrial banking, must obviously become integral parts of the Guild organisation, and the Banking System must obviously be under the control of the Guilds which it would have to finance.   If the Guild arguments apply to one capitalistic industry or service, they apply to all, and their democracy is just as necessary for a distributive or commercial as for a productive group of workers.

Assuming, then, the existence of largely decentralised National Guilds covering all the vital industries and services, let us see how these Guilds would be related one to another. While all forms of production and economic service are, in the last resort, undertaken for the benefit of the ultimate user or consumer, a great part of both is actually of an intermediate character.   The greater part of the product of the iron and steel or of the coal industry, for example, goes, not directly to the ultimate consumer, but to other industries which use it for purposes of further production or service. Similarly, the transport industries, while they carry millions of passengers and of personal packages belonging to passengers, are even more engaged in carrying goods which will only reach the consumer, if at all, through the intermediacy of another industry.   Of the total volume of exchange, therefore, under a Guild system as under any other, a large percentage would take place between one industry or service and another.   That is, there would be an immense mutual traffic among the Guilds. Moreover, the relations between Guilds would vary widely in closeness and importance from case to case.   The transport and manufacturing industries, for example, would all have very close and constant relations with the coal industry, and nearly all the industries making finished products would have very close relations with the distributive industry.   On the other hand, the pottery and cotton industries would have few, if any, direct points of contact with each other.

Clearly, where two or more Guilds stood in a close and constant mutual relationship of this character, there would have to be specially close connections established between them.   Each would require on its staff experts who understood the technique of the others, and there would have to be special joint committees, and probably—the equivalent of some interlocking directorates of to-day—mutual exchange of seats on the governing bodies of the Guilds. And all this network of mutual relationships would exist fully as much locally and regionally as it would nationally ; for the need of avoiding centralisation extends quite as much to the processes of exchange and to inter-Guild relations as to production.   The Guilds would establish relations and negotiate exchange to a great extent locally, and probably particular factories belonging to different Guilds would often establish direct relations and work by the method of direct exchange.

In addition to this close relationship between individual Guilds and parts of Guilds, under which each Guild and its parts would probably enter into a vast variety of special connections, there would be co-ordination and common action among the whole body of the industrial Guilds.   This brings us to our first consideration of the Congress of Industrial Guilds, and of its place in the Guild structure.   Its wider place in the organisation of Society as a whole we cannot consider until we have completed our picture of the other forms of essential association in the Guild community.

The Industrial Guilds Congress, successor to the Trades Union Congress of to-day, would represent directly every Guild concerned with industry or economic service.[1]   It too would have its local and regional counterparts in local and regional Guild Councils, successors to the Trades Councils and Federations of Trades Councils which now exist.   And again, in order that the tendency to a centralising point of view may be avoided, these local Councils, or at least the regional Councils representative of them, should be directly represented in the Industrial Guilds Congress.   The local point

[1] It might also well include representatives from the enterprises organised on essentially Guild lines, but not included in a National Guild.

of view will require to be strongly put, and, since the bulk of inter-Guild exchange will be likely to take place locally, these Local Guild Councils will clearly be bodies of very great economic importance.

The Industrial Guilds Congress, to some extent as the central Trade Union body is reported to be in Russia to-day, would be the final representative body of the Guild system on its industrial side, and would have the vital function of laying down and interpreting the essential principles of Guild organisation and practice. It would be, in fact, on questions requiring central co-ordination, the Guild legislature, and, either itself or through a subordinate organ, the ultimate court of appeal on purely Guild questions. Many of its most important functions cannot be discussed until we come to consider it in its relations to other bodies in the community; but we can say here that it would act as the representative of the Guilds as a whole in their common external relations, both with other parts of the body social, and with Guild and other organisations abroad. One of its functions, but by no means among the most important, would be to adjudicate on inter-Guild difficulties and disputes, the local Guild Councils acting as normal courts of first instance on such questions. But its most important internal Guild function would be that of laying down the general principles of Guild conduct, in the form of general regulations within which each Guild would have to work.

This brings us very close indeed to a problem which has probably been for some time in the readers' mind. How is the pay of the individual Guildsman, and of the various grades of workers in a Guild, to be determined, and how is the level of payment as between the various Guilds to be adjusted?

One of the most important tasks entrusted to the central Trade Union organisation in Russia has been that of drawing up, on the advice of the various Unions, elaborate schedules of payment for almost every conceivable class of industrial workers. We may hope that the need for quite such detailed regulation will not present itself in a Guild Society; but clearly a closely analogous function will fall to the Industrial Guilds Congress. If we assume any inequality of payment to continue—and to this point we shall come shortly—clearly the levels of remuneration to be paid to different classes of workers will need to be regulated, at any rate in general terms, by some central body. Guildsmen used to hold that one way of dealing with this question would be to allow each Guild to allocate to its salary fund a sum exactly proportionate to the number of its members, and to divide this sum among them as it might choose; but I am now doubtful whether this method would be practicable, at any rate in the earlier stages. The alternative seems to be for the salary scales drawn up by each Guild to be subject to review and modification by the Guilds Congress, which will be in a position to adjust the claims of various sections of workers.   In suggesting this, I am not losing sight of the fact that other associations besides industrial Guilds may have a close concern and claim to a voice in the salaries to be paid.   I admit this claim, and deal with the point later in discussing the working of Guild Society as a communal system.[2]   Here I am only discussing what seems to me a practical method of arriving at a fair balance between the various groups of producers.

But, in taking up this attitude, have I not assumed the case against equality of income? Yes—and yet, emphatically, no.   I assume indeed that equality of income cannot, and must not, be made a condition of the establishment of the Guild system; for I am convinced that the moral and psychological conditions which would make such equality possible could develop only in the atmosphere of a free Society, and even there only by a gradual process.   It is essentially true that equality, if it proves, as I think it must, the only solution of the problem of income, can only develop out of the actual experience of free and democratic industrial and social conditions; and I am sure that, when it does come, it will come, not in the absurd guise of " equality of remuneration," but by the destruction of the whole idea of remuneration for work done, and the apprehension of the economic problem as that of dividing the national income, without regard to any particular work or service, among the members of the community. On this point, at any rate, Bernard Shaw is right.

Until the consciousness arises that will make this change possible, some inequalities of remuneration are likely to persist, although it is quite possible, and indeed most likely, that particular factories or Guilds, seizing the essential justice of equality and realising the impossibility of attempting to measure in economic rewards the respective values of different kinds of service, will take the initiative in adopting equality for their own members. Their decisions will pass through the Guilds Congress with the rest, and will have their influence in leavening the whole.

In addition to the problem of pay, the Guilds Congress will have to survey, from the point of view of all the Guilds, the whole field of economic conditions. We can best see wherein its essential work of laying down and raising the standard of conditions for all the Guilds will consist by examining, in its general outlines, the status and economic position of the worker engaged in Guild industry. Wherein, apart from the factory and industrial democracy which we have discussed already,

will his position in industry differ from that of
the wage-worker of to-day?   One obvious
difference is that unemployment, or rather loss
of employment, as it now exists, will have
disappeared.   There will be no such thing as
a Guildsman who has lost his income because,
owing to slackness of work, he is out of a job,
or has had it drastically reduced because, from
the same cause, he is working short time.
Every Guildsman will be assured of his full
income from the Guild whatever the " state of
the market," and, apart from other factors
which will cause the present fluctuations of
trade to be greatly modified, this fact will be an
immense force in steadying the demand for
commodities and services.   Every Guildsman
will be " on the strength " of his Guild in sickness as well as in health ; and he will thus have
gained one thing which the wage-worker most
manifestly lacks to-day—economic security—
and have gained it not by submitting to slavery
(the slave has security of a sort) ; but as a con-
comitant of industrial freedom.

Secondly, the Guildsman will have become,
to a great extent, his own industrial law-giver.
He will have the sense of being an active parti-
cipator in an industrial system based on the
social recognition of free service.   He will not
have to fear for his old age, or for his children's
future ; for his service will ensure to him maintenance at his standard when he retires, and
before his children there will be an assured

place in a system open to all.   For the Guilds
will be, not closed corporations, but open
associations which any man may join; and,
should need arise, it will be one of the chief
duties of the Industrial Guilds Congress and
indeed of the whole community, to preserve the
open door into the Guilds, and the career open
to merit up to the highest and most responsible
positions in them.   This does not mean, of
course, that any person will be able to claim
admission, as an absolute right, into the Guild
of his choice.   In many occupations, there will
be preliminary training, apprenticeship and
tests of fitness to be passed, and it will be the
business of the Congress to ensure the fairness
of such tests, if it is challenged.   Moreover, a
man clearly cannot get into a Guild unless it
needs fresh recruits for its work.   He will have
free choice, but only of the available openings.
The Congress, however, will have, in case of
need, to assure itself that no Guild is restricting
its numbers, or refusing applicants, from any
ulterior motive.   There will be, in essence,
free choice of occupation.

But we must meet the inevitable question,
" Who will do the dirty work under Guild
Socialism?" There have always been Socialists
who have favoured, for such work, a period of
industrial conscription for everybody.   I am
opposed to this, and I think nearly all Guildsmen are opposed to it.   I am opposed first,
and most of all, because I do not want Guild

Society to be based at any point on sheer
coercion, but also because I am sure that the
system would operate badly and unfairly.   It
is, moreover, unnecessary.   Let us first by the
fullest application of machinery and scientific
methods eliminate or reduce to the narrowest
limits all the forms of " dirty work " that admit
of such treatment.   This has never been tried ;
for, under capitalism, " dirty work " is the
last thing to which invention is usually applied.
It is cheaper to exploit and ruin human beings.
This method would produce enormous results.
Secondly, let us see what forms of " dirty
work " we can do without, and make up our
minds definitely that, if any form of work is
not only unpleasant but degrading, we will do
without it, whatever the cost.   No human
being ought to be either allowed or compelled
to do work that degrades.   Thirdly, for what
dull or unpleasant work remains, let us offer
whatever special conditions are required to
attract the necessary workers, not in higher
pay, but in shorter hours, holidays extending
over six months in the year, conditions attrac-
tive enough to men who have other uses for
their time or attention to bring the requisite
number to undertake it voluntarily.   Under
such conditions the doing of this work will fall,
not to the outcasts of Society, but to men
whose lives are so full of desires to do unpaid
work in their own individual way that they
choose to earn their livings by doing dull work

for a brief part of their time, as many an original writer takes to hack journalism to-day.[3]

3 The alternative would be better; for it would not spoil his style.

CHAPTER V

THE CONSUMER

Who is the "consumer"? Some say he is Mr. Everybody, and therefore entitled to all power and consideration. Others say that, being Mr. Everybody, he is also Mr. Nobody, and can be safely left out of account. In other words, some social theorists, as we saw in the second chapter, base their economic scheme on the consumer, on the ground that all production is directed to the satisfaction of needs, and that needs are everybody's lot; while others base their scheme on the producer, on the ground that all production is the result of service, and that with responsibilities and active functions should go power and control.

I have already tried to explain why I cannot accept either of these views in its entirety. I believe that, in a very real sense, it is "more blessed to give than to receive," and that the emphasis of social organisation should therefore be on service rather than on common interest; but this is a very different matter from ignoring the common interests of consumers altogether, or reducing their expression to a quite subordinate place in Society.

But have consumers a common interest? This is sometimes denied. It is stated that, while there may be a common interest and point of view among a particular kind of consumers or users of a particular kind of product or service, there is no such thing as a common point of view of all consumers and users of all kinds of goods and services. On this view, particular groups of consumers have a reality and a claim to consideration; but "the consumer" as such is a mirage.

In the case of the producers, details apart, the lines of division and the bond of unity are alike clear enough. Production falls fairly naturally into a number of distinct groups or services, and at the same time the common character in all service, and the common element in the point of view of all who serve, stand out distinctly. On the other hand, generally speaking, we are all, or we should be in an equalitarian community, more or less consumers of everything. Consumers are thus not split up into a number of groups of individuals, one group consuming one product and one another.

There is one school of thought that will say

that this impossibility of sorting consumers out into groups is the best possible indication of their essential unity, and of the reality of "the consumer." But this is to ignore the vital principle on which social organisation ought to proceed—the principle of function. The fact that, more or less, everybody combines in himself all forms of consumption does not prove that all these forms can be regarded as parts of a single function of his—"consumption as a whole"; for he also combines in himself many other concerns—his concern as a producer, for example—which clearly form no part of "consumption." The question, then, is not whether everybody consumes everything, or whether the consumer is "Mr. Everybody," but whether consumption, taken as a whole, forms a coherent social interest or group of interests corresponding to production, and, if so, whether it possesses any principle of internal differentiation analogous to, however different from, the internal differentiation of forms of production.

I believe that "consumption" does form in a real sense a coherent group of interests, and that it does possess an essential principle of differentiation. But I do not believe that any real representation of consumers will be secured unless this principle of internal differentiation is observed, any more than producers would be properly represented if all production were treated as an undifferentiated mass. What, then, is this principle?

We have seen that this distinction cannot coincide with any distinction of individuals. A man is usually either a miner or a railway-man, and not both; but he consumes coal, uses the railways, and only limits the variety of his consumption by his lack of opportunity. But in both the essential social differentiation is not that between individuals but that between interests or concerns, that is, between types of production and consumption.

It is surely fairly clear, as soon as we adopt this basis, that consumption—in which I in-clude the use of economic services—falls into two main divisions, which may admit of fur-ther sub-division. The first division includes consumption of a household or individual type, and extends roughly over all the ordinary forms of purchase covered by the term " shop-ping." In this type of consumption, the in-dividual purchaser or the housewife sallies forth to buy commodities, in the purchase of which there is generally a good deal of room for individual choice and variety of purchase. One housewife prefers a " Ewbank " and another a " Star Vacuum Cleaner ": one smoker fancies cut plug and another John Cotton; and these differences are matters of taste and opinion fully as much as of price. For convenience, we shall call this first division of consumption " personal and domestic consumption."

The second division includes all those forms of use or consumption in which, although the individual may choose whether to use them or not and in what particular quantity he will use them, the product itself is undifferentiated, and is supplied in the mass. I may decide whether or not, or whither, to travel by railway or train; but I cannot, at least under democratic conditions, order a special railway or train. I may cut down or increase my consumption of water or electricity; but I cannot order a special kind. Let us call this second division of consumption " collective consumption." These collective utility services are in most cases of such a nature as to require monopolistic control.

Of course, there are all kinds of cases falling on the border-line between those two divisions. For example, is bread differentiated or undifferentiated? Both it and milk fall on the border-line. Bread, however, is closely connected with other forms of confectionery and foodstuffs, and therefore most naturally assimilates itself to the domestic group. Milk and butter probably go the same way. Gas, on the other hand, and coal are consumed in the home; but they are both so largely undifferentiated products and are so largely used in connection with other collective services, that they naturally assimilate themselves to the collective group. The marginal cases, in fact, can be placed on either side of the division according to convenience.

The attempt to establish this principle of differentiation of forms of consumption is by no means an arbitrary exercise of theoretical ingenuity, but has a very direct bearing on the whole question of the place of the consumer in Society. For a concentration of attention mainly on consumption of the first type has produced the school of thought which looks to the Co-operative Movement as the essential protagonist of the consumer, while a concentration on the second type has produced Collectivism, especially in the form of Municipal Socialism.

As we saw in an earlier chapter, both the State and Municipal Socialists and those idealists who believe that the future industrial system will be based on an extension of the method of Co-operative trading to all industries and services[1] found their proposals on a claim that "the consumer" must control. But, whereas it is quite clear that the Co-operators set out with their practical experience of organising one form of consumption and the Collectivists with the working of nationalised and municipalised services mainly

---

[1] Such as the Women's Co-operative Guild, and Mr. L. S. Woolf in his book, *Co-operation and the Future of Industry.* It should be noted that the Co-operative Movement as a whole is not necessarily committed to this view.

in mind, the thorough-going advocates of
either system are not as a rule inclined to
attach any greater importance to the distinction between the two main forms of consumption.   The Collectivists carry resolutions
calling for the nationalisation of all the means
of production, distribution and exchange, and
thus lay themselves open to the charge, recently made by Mr. Asquith during the
Paisley bye-election, of wishing to nationalise
the Co-operative Movement, while the Co-
operativists dwell on the dangers of handing
over industry to be run by " political " bodies,
and stress the inadequacy of such bodies in
representing the consumer. The two theories
thus evidently come into sharp conflict with
each other, while both come into conflict, at
a different point, with the theory of Guild
Socialism.

For the moment, we are concerned, not
with this latter conflict, but with the rival
claims of the Co-operative Movement and of
the State and the Local Authority to represent the consumer. It seems clear that there
are certain points which follow immediately
on the principles which we laid down at the
beginning of this book. Whatever may be
the shortcomings of Co-operation to-day, its
claim to be at least capable of serving as the
basis for a true representation of consumers
in their personal and domestic capacity must
be admitted to be fully as strong as the claim

of the Trade Unions to be capable of serving as the basis for National Guilds. For Co-operation, like Trade Unionism, is a great spontaneous movement of the working-class, and has always set before it the clear and definite function of representing the claim of the working-class consumer, especially in relation to goods of personal or domestic use.

Secondly, it seems clear that the Co-operativist contention that the representation of the consumer cannot properly, in a democratic Society, be entrusted to a " political " body is sound, and follows immediately upon the functional principle which we laid down at the outset. The representation of the consumer, whether generally or in relation to any particular type of consumption, must be a specific, functional, *ad hoc* representation, and this is not secured by entrusting it, as an additional responsibility, to a body which is primarily political. But it does not follow from this that the Co-operativists, in destroying " political " nationalisation, have established their own exclusive claim; for it seems clear that the functional principle would still be violated if all " consumption " were treated as an undifferentiated mass, and its representation assigned to a single body. The questions and points of view which emerge, and the outlook and capacity required, are different in the case of personal and domestic consumption on the one hand, and " collective " consumption on the other, and different forms of representation and organisation are accordingly required for their expression.

This leads us to the necessity of making a further distinction. It is clear that "the State," the national governmental machine, is primarily and essentially a political body, and therefore cannot be a proper representative of any form of consumption. But does this apply, in the same sense, to the local authorities? It is, I agree, clear that the local authorities, in their present form, are not suitable representatives of consumption; but this is not so much because they are "political" as because they are not only perverted by class antagonism, but also attempt to combine, with the economic function of representing consumers, certain other functions which are neither economic nor political, but essentially civic. By this I mean functions connected with such services as education, public health, and civic amenities generally, which certainly cannot be properly brought under either the economic or the political category. A fuller treatment of these civic services, in relation both to those who render service in them and to those who use and enjoy them, must be reserved for the following chapter in which the Civic Guilds are discussed. But here we can already establish the point that the combination of "civic" and collectivist functions in a single body is manifestly wrong in principle, and in complete violation of the whole functional basis on which we are working.

Let us assume, then, that the duties of the present Local Authorities have been divided among two or more bodies, and that one of these bodies, which we may call the "Collective Utilities Council," has assigned to it only functions of a definitely economic character. As soon as this is the case, the argument against the Local Authority as a representative of consumption fails, and it becomes fully as proper and natural a representative of "the consumer" in relation to collective consumption as the Co-operative Movement is in relation to personal and domestic consumption.

We thus arrive at the conclusions, first, that consumers' representation is essential; secondly, that Co-operation, or some form of organisation arising out of it, is the proper representative of the consumer in relation to personal and domestic consumption; and, thirdly, that the "Collective Utilities Council," inheriting a part of the functions of the Local Authority of to-day, is the consumers' proper representative in relation to collective consumption as we have defined it.

This brings us back to the question, of which we have already undertaken a preliminary discussion in Chapter II, of the proper relations, under a democratic industrial system, between the Guilds, as representatives of the producers, and the future Co-operative Movement and the Collective Utilities Council, as representatives of the consumers. It has already been made clear that, in the Guild Socialist view, the consumers' claim and interest does not properly extend to the direct management of industry, which would involve a servile status for the producer, but to the safeguarding of certain specific concerns of the consumer, mainly in connection with quantity and quality of production, adequacy of distribution to meet volume and variety of needs, and price of sale, with other closely related concerns.

Since we discussed this point, we have set forth as clearly as possible the internal working both of a Guild, and of the Guilds as a whole. We are now therefore, with the organisation on both producers' and consumers' behalf in our minds, able to discuss, in a more concrete way, the desirable relations between them.

It is clear, from what we have said already, that the normal conduct of each industry and service is placed in the hands of a Guild, and that the best chance for the consumers of securing really efficient, because willing and communally inspired, service is to leave the producer as far as possible to manage his own affairs. The essence of the whole proposal is that the producers, as an organised profession, should be put " on their honour " to do their best, and should feel that every action which they perform well is a direct and useful contribution which they freely make to the service of the community. The relation of the consumer and his representatives to a service so organised is essentially not antagonistic but complementary. The main function of the consumers' organisation is to make articulate and definite the consumers' needs and desires, in the expectation, not that the producer will seek to thwart them, but that he will be eager to elicit and respond to them because he will have the strongest of social motives for doing so, and no sufficient motive for doing otherwise. The secondary function of protecting the consumer against the producer will therefore only come exceptionally into play, and it is a great mistake to conceive of it as the main reason for providing for consumers' representation. The provision for such protection requires to be strong and adequate; but, if the system works properly, it will be seldom invoked. The real reason for consumers' representation is that the '' consuming '' point of view requires to be definitely expressed, in order that articulate demand may co-operate with, and direct the course of, organised supply.

I conceive, then, of the dual form of consumers' organisation—Co-operative and Collective—existing in every town and village and probably in every ward and hamlet, and

of the consumers' representatives meeting
constantly for discussion with the Guild representatives. It is no less essential that consumers', than that Guild, organisation should
be strongly decentralised and vigorously local
in its life, and the real democracy of it depends
no less on beginning with, and building up
from, the smallest natural unit of consumers'
common action and feeling. The internal
structure of the consumers' organisations,
Collective as well as Co-operative, should follow essentially the same principles as the Guild
organisation which has been already described.
It should begin with the self-government of
the small unit, and create its larger regional
and national organisation by the bringing together of the representatives of these units.
The Co-operative Movement already does this
to a considerable extent ; and the creation of
Collective Utilities Councils to assume the
economic functions of the local authorities
should not stop short with the town, but
should be carried further by the formation,
on the same basis, of regional Collective Utilities Councils drawn from the local Councils
and of a National Council drawn from the
regional bodies. This National Collective
Utilities Council would be, whereas the State
is not and cannot be, a proper national representative of collective consumption.

The Guild Socialist system makes, then, the
fullest provision for joint consultation and

action between the Guilds and the consumers'
organisations at every stage, local, regional
and national. This would take the form both
of direct relations between a particular Guild,
or section of a Guild, and either the appropriate Co-operative or the appropriate " Collective " body, and also of direct relations
between all the Guilds concerned with the
" Co-operative " group of services and the
Co-operative body, all the Guilds concerned
with the " Collective " services and the Collective body, and the whole body of Guilds
and both consumers' bodies. Moreover, all
these contacts could take place at any stage,
local, regional, or national. We have thus a
second set of inter-relations, this time between
producers and consumers, following upon the
inter-Guild relations which we have already
described.

But, I can hear my reader asking, what
would be the *powers* of the consumers' bodies,
if the Guilds were firmly entrenched in the
control of the various industries and services?
Could not the producers, relying on their
economic power, merely ignore the consumers'
representations, and follow their own sweet
will? The answer to that vital question can
only be given when we have discussed not only
the Guilds and the consumers' organisation,
but the *communal* structure of Guild Society
as a whole, that is, the relations, within the
community, of all the various forms of func-

tional organisation. I must therefore ask the
reader to have patience a little longer, and let
me get the description of the vital organs of
Guild Society complete by means of the next
chapter. Then we can come to the vexed
question of power and of the interaction and
communal expression of functional democracy.
The point is not being lost sight of; but it can
only be dealt with in its proper place.

But, before I leave the question of the consumer, there is a further point with which it
is necessary to deal. Throughout this chapter,
I have used the word " consumption " only in
its proper and limited sense, as applying to the
ultimate consumption or use of products or
services for the direct satisfaction of human
needs or desires. That is to say, I have not
dealt with all the various forms of so-called
" intermediate consumption " which were discussed in the last chapter under the heading
of inter-Guild relations. When a railway or
a ship uses coal, or when a factory orders new
machinery or buildings, the " consumer," in
so far as there is one, is the industry requiring
the product. The direct representative of this
" quasi-consumption " is therefore the Guild
of that industry, and the representation of this
form of " consumption " is secured through
the inter-Guild relations already described. It
is, however, manifestly the case that the ultimate consumer, although he does not consume
the coal or the machinery or the buildings, is

very closely affected by their supply, quality, price and distribution, since these things directly affect the supply, quality, price and distribution of the goods which he does actually consume. It is therefore clear that relations must exist between the consumers' representatives, Collective and Co-operative, and the Guilds producing for "intermediate consumption" as well as between the consumers and the Guilds producing final products or rendering direct services. Thus, all the Guilds would be represented in the Joint Councils of producers and consumers as a whole, and a consumers' body could claim representation and facilities for consultation and common action in relation to any Guild with whose working it was concerned, whether the concern with its products was direct or indirect.

Again, it is exceedingly probable that, in relation to certain services, such as railway travelling, there would spring up special *ad hoc* associations of consumers or users of a particular type of product or service. There are, in some places to-day, not only Railway Season Ticket Holders' Associations, but also Telephone Users' Associations and other similar bodies. The continuance and extension of such organisations, and special provision for their representation in relation to the appropriate Guilds, is thoroughly desirable and fully consistent with the functional principle of democracy. It is also likely that there would exist consumers' associations of a smaller and more special type, formed for the purpose of co-operation with special groups of craftsmen or for the encouragement of special types of product, and these would form an obviously desirable complement to the independent producers' organisations whose continued existence, in certain special cases, we have agreed to be a valuable source of craft initiative and variety in production.

The importance, from a practical point of view, of the conclusions reached in this chapter is sufficiently evident. It means, first, that, so far from there being any antagonism between the Co-operative Movement and Guild Socialism, the rapid extension of Co-operation to supply, as nearly as possible, the personal and domestic needs of the whole population is a development of democratic organisation which Guildsmen ought to make every effort to advance. It means, secondly, that the reform and re-organisation of the Local Government of this country ought to be taken immediately and vigorously in hand, with a view to the separation of its civic and economic functions, and that, both as a means to this end and in order to make full use of it when it has been reorganised, Labour ought to follow up its recent advance in local elections by making a determined effort to secure

the complete control of Local Government
for the organised workers.

NOTE.—It is, I hope, no longer necessary to deal with the argument
that. because producers and consumers are the same persons, there is no
need for distinct organisations to represent the respective points of view.
Play used to be made with this argument both by Collectivists, who
said that Guilds were unnecessary because the State represented everybody and State Socialism would therefore be industrial democracy, and
by Industrial Unionists, who said that, since in a democratic Society
all consumers would be producers, producers' control would amply
represent the consumer. These two arguments always had a most
convenient way of cancelling out, and their advocates for the most part
retired hurt some time ago. It is, I think, clear that a person requires
as many forms of representation as he has distinct organisable interests
or points of view.

CHAPTER VI

THE CIVIC SERVICES

WE have been dealing, so far, entirely with Guild Socialism as a scheme of industrial and economic organisation, and have not, except incidentally, touched upon its application to services of a non-economic character. But it must be obvious that the arguments which have been advanced in favour of self-government in industry apply at least equally to those services whose purpose is, not the satisfaction of economic wants, but the fulfilment of spiritual, mental, and other non-economic needs and desires. The necessity of evoking, in these essentially civic services, the spirit of free communal devotion is at least as great, and the opportunity is, by reason of their character, greater and more easily seized than in the case of most economic activities. If there is anywhere a real chance for free organisation conceived in the spirit of public service, it is surely in such spheres as education and health, in which there is, even under their present depressing conditions, considerable scope for idealistic motives and devoted endeavour.

It is true that the conditions under which such professions as those of teaching and medicine are now carried on have resulted, to a considerable extent, in their assimilation to the economic services, and their infection by the spirit of greed, grab and acquisitive struggle by which these are at present dominated. But it is recognised even now that this spirit is foreign to the real nature of the civic services, and ineffectual protests are raised from time to time against their tendency to acquire a capitalistic character. These protests are, of course, directed chiefly against underpaid teachers and overworked general practitioners who are compelled to assume an acquisitive attitude in the desperate attempt to make both ends meet. They have, nevertheless, a real basis in the recognition of the essentially non-economic character of the services in question. They are, however, and must continue to be ineffectual as long as the industrial conditions, to which their own are inevitably assimilated, remain under the domination of capitalism and capitalist morality. Their rescue from their present degradation will only proceed side by side with the rescue of the economic system from the even worse degradation into which it has fallen.

7

I propose, in this chapter, to concentrate attention mainly upon one of these services, which seems to me, by reason of its social purpose, to be the most important of all. Education, as advocates of revolution are mostly tired of being reminded, to a great extent conditions the possibility of all change for the better. Democracy, we are constantly told, is only possible for an educated people, and, even if this is only true on the broadest interpretation of what education means, it is most certainly the case that the character of the educational system goes far towards determining the mental outlook and capacity for freedom of the citizens. An education that is rightly conceived in such a way as to elicit, in child and adult alike, the fullest possible capacity for initiative and self-expression, will make easy for the people feats of self-government and communal expression which would be quite beyond the reach of a people educated under a routine system making for servility and unquestioning obedience that reasons not why.

It will not, I think, be disputed that our public educational system, under which the great majority of the nation are brought up, is to a great extent a servile system. It is not, perhaps, quite so servile as it has been, and recent reforms will make a further slight improvement. But no mere addition to the quantity of education provided, and no mere raising of the school age, will fundamentally alter the character of the system.

This servility of present educational arrangements is traced by its critics to various causes. Some dwell, quite rightly, on the inordinate size of the classes which the unfortunate teacher is called upon to teach, and point out, with perfect truth, that it is impossible to communicate education to a mob. But the size of classes, while it is a serious aggravation of the servility of the system, is not the root cause of its servility. Other critics are content to say that the system is servile because it is capitalist, and it is to the interest of capitalists to train contented wage-slaves. This is certainly true; but it only drives us back to the further problem of the means by which capitalism succeeds in imparting this servile character to what should be a great agent of spiritual enfranchisement. The fundamental answer, I think, is to be found in the present status and equipment of the teacher, who is, under existing conditions, as much a wage-slave as any hireling of the industrial system, and worse exploited than most. The teacher is afforded only a quite inadequate and often inferior training, sometimes in a University, but more often in an institution that is not quite as good as a University. He or she, with this shoddy equipment, is then pitchforked into a school, and told to teach, under the supervision of a horde of inspectors, according

to Board of Education instructions, under the
control of an Education Authority whose
members usually know nothing about education, and in an atmosphere of jealousy created
directly by the dire economic distress of the
teacher, and the scarcity of promotions carrying a reasonable salary or reasonable opportunities. It is no wonder at all that, under
these conditions, very many teachers can be
accused of being " narrow-minded " and not
too efficient. They would be miracles if they
were otherwise, and, in the circumstances, the
work which many of them do is little short of
miraculous. But there is a limit to miracles;
and the majority of teachers are human beings,
and many have come to be teachers, not because they have a vocation for teaching, but
because, in the present scramble, even the
worst-paid professions have some economic
attractions superior to those of starvation or
mercenary marriage.

The only way of changing the character of
the educational system is by changing the
status of the teacher; for the teachers alone
can purify education, and they can do so only
if the conditions enable them to make a beginning. We shall set our feet on the right
road in respect of education only when we
make teaching a fully self-governing profession; and we shall get a good and liberating
educational system only when we have helped
the teachers to use their freedom to purge

education of its present capitalistic and economic taint.

We need, then, in so far as our educational system is to be regarded as a single unit, an Education Guild, in which the teachers will possess a self-governing status fully equivalent to that of the economic workers in one of the Guilds which we have already described. And, in the same way, we need a Guild of Health and a Guild for every civic service that ministers to an essential non-economic need of the people.

When I say that we need an Education Guild, or a Health Guild, I want the reader to bear in mind what I have said already about the essentially decentralised character of the Guild system, and the need for basing self-government on the smallest natural units of control. There is no sphere in which the hand of centralised large-scale organisation is likely to be so deadening, just as there is none in which the hand of bureaucracy is so deadening to-day, as that of the civic and essentially spiritual services with which we are now dealing. There is nowhere such need for variety, for diverse initiative and multiform experiment, for freedom to develop individual ideas and peculiar notions, as in this sphere on which so much of human happiness depends. Therefore, if we build up our educational and our health services into great national systems, and express their unity in great National

Guilds including all their different forms and stages, we must preserve within these large organisations the seat of power and the initiation of policy in the small units, so that each school may be as free as possible to strike out new lines for itself, and so that the initiative of individual medical men, or groups of fellow-workers, may not be hampered by too much central control.

In the case of education, which we are using throughout the chapter to illustrate the general principle, this involves the fullest admission of the right, which we have already recognised in the case of industry, of individuals or groups, on conforming with the most elementary regulations, to make experiments outside as well as inside the regular and recognised educational system. We may hope, indeed, as we hoped in the case of industry, that the spirit of freedom will be so fully developed in the National Guild that the great majority of new experiments will be able to take place within it; but the idea of an educational monopoly, however loose, is abhorrent, and there will always be experiments for which a national system, however elastic, will fail to find a place. Most of these may be " quackeries "; but it is better to admit many quackeries than to boycott one real educational discovery, and the danger of quackeries would be greatly reduced if, in the ways suggested later, the pupils secured a measure of self-government as well as the teachers.

Our Education Guild, then, must be even more decentralised than the majority of the productive Guilds, and must be much more a consultative federation of interrelated free educational institutions than a single unitary organisation. Under these conditions, it must, of course, include the institutions responsible for education at all its stages—from primary school to University, as we say to-day.[1] For our insistence on freedom does not mean isolation, either of the particular school or college or of a particular stage in the educational process. The extent to which education is isolated, not only by class divisions, but also by stages, to-day is one of the worst features of the present system. We require to look at the educational problem as a single whole, without allowing ourselves to be led into the error of centralising it because we recognise its unity.

A National Education Guild, including many diverse types of teachers with varying techniques, methods and functions, will clearly require, in its internal organisation, highly diversified democratic forms. There will have to be provision for self-government not only in the school, where it is most important of

[1] Of course, much education would take place outside any organised educational system—in the home, and in voluntary associations of children for all manner of purposes

all, and in the larger areas of educational administration, but also in the various professional and " craft " groups comprehended in the teaching profession. And, in addition to the diverse provision for group expression made in the Guild itself, locally as well as nationally, there will be required the fullest freedom of voluntary professional association and of recognition for such forms of association. A simple instance of what I mean is furnished by the problem of qualifying tests for teachers themselves. It would be a great mistake for the National Guild to attempt to concentrate in its own hands the whole function of applying such tests to entrants to the profession or aspirants to its higher qualifications. It would be far better, wherever possible, for the Guild to delegate or entrust to various professional and similar bodies the task of deciding, within limits, on the qualifications of candidates. This, as we have seen already, would be the proper method for the economic Guilds to adopt in many cases in relation to the industrial professions, and it clearly applies with at least equal force in the case both of the educational and of the medical services.

Before we attempt to forecast in greater detail the internal organisation of the Education Guild, there are two fundamental problems, both connected with its relation to other parts of the communal structure, that require to be discussed. What will be the

relation of the Guild, in respect of education
generally, to the body of citizens, and more
particularly to those citizens of to-day and to-
morrow who come to its institutions as pupils
or students?   And what will be its relation,
especially in connection with technical education, to the various economic Guilds and
professional associations?

These two problems are in some degree
analogous to, but in no respect the same as,
certain problems which we have discussed already in relation to the economic Guilds.
There is resemblance, but certainly not identity, between our first problem and the problem of the economic Guilds and the consumer,
and there is a resemblance, perhaps less close
but still real, between the second and that of
intermediate " consumption " and inter-Guild
relations.   But there is, in the case of education and also, to only a slightly less extent,
in that of health, the vital difference that the
services in question are not economic services,
and that the character of the service provided
raises spiritual and moral problems of immense
social consequence.   When we propose internally self-governing Guilds for education
and health, we are clearly not suggesting that
all questions of education and health should be
left to be determined wholly by the teachers
or the doctors.   Both education and health are
matters in which every citizen is intimately
concerned, and upon which he must be assured

of the fullest opportunity of bringing his opinion and influence to bear. The other Guilds and the professional associations, again, are clearly concerned most vitally in the questions of technical education, and here their voice, as well as that of the teacher and of the ordinary citizen, must be able to make itself effectively heard.

In our discussion of Local Government in its economic aspects, we have already made it clear that, if local authorities are to be fitted for the necessary function of representing the "collective" consumer, there must be separate bodies, constituted and elected for this purpose alone and not attempting to combine it with non-economic purposes. But, if this is essential from the economic point of view, how much more obviously necessary is it from the standpoint of the civic services which we are now discussing; for clearly the liberation of these services from their subjection to economics can hardly be even attempted as long as they remain under the control of bodies which almost inevitably put first in their thoughts the economic point of view. We require, then, side by side with the Collective Utilities Councils described in the last chapter, other Councils which will express the needs and desires of the people in relation to the civic services. Nor would the case be met by a simple division into two of the local authorities; for the necessity which we have recog-

nised for at least two distinct forms of organisation, the Co-operative and the Collective, to represent the different divisions of
consumption, is far more than reproduced in
the case of the civic services, which fall into
groups far more clearly distinct in their main
characteristics than any two or more economic
groups can be. If we take only the two great
services which we have so far been discussing
—education and public health—it is clear that,
although these overlap and interpenetrate at
many points, both with each other and with
various forms of economic service, they present
in each case a distinct and separate body of
problems which demands distinct treatment
and calls for quite distinct qualifications and
interests on the part of those who are to represent the public point of view in relation to
it.   Education and health cannot, then, if
we are to adhere to our functional principle,
be assigned to the same bodies ; and we must
pronounce in favour of a return to the *ad hoc*
method of administration which Collectivist
reformers, failing to recognise the difference
between economic and civic services, have been
so busy destroying in recent times.

We need, then, in every locality, side by
side with the Collective Utilities Council, a
Council to deal, from the point of view of the
whole body of citizens, with educational questions, and another to deal with health questions. This, however, does not point the way

to an indefinite multiplication of distinct *ad hoc* Local Authorities; for the proper conception of the functions of education and health is far wider than that which dominates public policy to-day. This distinction is so important that, at any rate in the case of education, it is probably best to mark it by a distinguishing word. Let us say, then, that for education in the widest sense, including many kindred spiritual services, we need *Cultural Councils* elected by all the citizens to express the civic point of view.

These Cultural Councils would enter into a close and constant relation, not only to the Education Guild, but to other Guilds providing kindred services. For example, the whole of the dramatic and musical professions and all concerned in the services which they provide, securing under a democratic social system the communal recognition extended to them by the people, but denied by the authorities, to-day, would, through their Guilds, be directly related to the Cultural Council which would exist to deal with their services fully as much as with education in the narrower sense of teaching. Art Galleries, Museums, Libraries and similar institutions, placed directly under the care of the Education Guild or of professional associations, would fall within the sphere of action of the Cultural Council. Again, the Health Council would be in direct relation not only to the

Medical Guild, but also to the Guilds organising the sanitary services, and would have in its sphere, as well as hospitals, parks and open spaces and other amenities of physical life. It would also have a close and constant, though not an exclusive, relation to the Building Guild, and would have a large voice in the determination of town-planning and region-planning policy.

As in the case of the Co-operative and Collective Councils, therefore, there would be, for the Health and Cultural Councils, a relation not to a single Guild, but to a group of cognate Guilds which would be themselves in close and constant interaction. It would also clearly be necessary for the Health and Cultural Councils and for the corresponding Guilds to enter into close connections for dealing jointly with problems common to both, such as the health of school children or the education of the mentally defective, so far as they continued after the abolition of economic destitution. They would also have to enter into relations, less close but still important, with the Collective and Co-operative Councils in respect of such questions as the milk supply, town-planning, educational facilities in relation to industry, and many others. Of this interrelation of the various forms of communal organisation we shall have more to say in the next chapter.

But, if this would be the structure of civic

representation in relation to these vital services, what would be the functions of the
representative Councils which we have described? As in the case of the economic
relationships described in the last chapter, it
would be essentially, not an antagonistic, but
a co-operative and complementary relationship. The Councils would exist to make articulate the civic point of view, the vital
spiritual and physical demands of the people,
and to co-operate with the various Guilds
which would have entrusted to them the task
of supplying these demands. There are
spiritual and physical as well as economic
demands, and in these spheres also articulate
demand must meet and co-operate with organised supply.

The Councils, then, would express the demand of the people, locally even more than
nationally, in accordance with the decentralisa-
tion of the system, in relation to cultural and
physical needs. The citizen is interested in
the type of education, drama, medical and
sanitary services, parks and public institutions
to be provided, and it is the business of those
whose vocation lies in these services to provide, in accordance with their knowledge and
initiative, what the people wants. It is sometimes argued that, especially in the sphere of
education, the majority of the people wants
nothing at all; but functional representation,
with the election of *ad hoc* authorities, very

properly gives those who do want something and do take an interest the best opportunity of making their voice heard. Moreover, under conditions of democratic equality of status, it is difficult to believe that the Cultural Council, with its opportunities for the expression of spiritual and artistic desires, would not provide the most popular of all openings for communal service.[2]

In the sphere of education, however, a further problem of civic expression now immediately confronts us. For, if the right of all adult citizens to vote for functional bodies provides a sufficient expression for the civic point of view in relation to health and some forms of cultural activity, what of that great part of education which is concerned with non-adults? Have not the child and the youth the right to make their voices heard in the moulding of the educational system, if not as a whole, at any rate where it touches them directly, in the school itself. I have no hesitation in recognising this right, and in saying that it must be provided for, not by a fantastic attempt to create large-scale representative machinery for non-adults, and still less by mixing up adults and non-adults on the Cultural Councils, but by providing, in every school, the fullest facilities for self-government

2 Again, we must reserve the special question of the relative *power* of these Councils and of the Guilds for consideration in the next chapter, which deals with the whole question of communal organisation under Guild Socialism

of the pupils as well as of the teachers. It has already been shown that the greatest experimental advances in this direction have been made in those schools in which the individual teachers themselves have enjoyed the fullest freedom and self-government, and I have no doubt that a general extension of freedom to the teachers would lead soon to a widespread developments of such experiments.[3] This self-government of the pupil would no doubt begin mainly in an increased control by boys and girls over their own affairs, including the greatest freedom of voluntary association in the school and substantial control over discipline; but it would rapidly extend to include, where necessary, actual criticism of the curriculum and the teacher, and co-operative suggestion of forms of study and methods of work. It is hardly possible to lay down rules or precepts for this development, which will take many different forms according to the individuality of the teacher and the spirit of the class; but, until a large measure of students' self-government is developed, democracy in the school will not be realised and the power of education as a liberating influence will not have been properly developed.

This brings us to the second big problem—that of technical education. There is to-day,

---

3 See *An Experiment in Educational Self-Government*, by J. B. Simpson, who is himself now concerned in a new school that is doing promising work on these lines.

owing to economic causes, constant friction
between advocates of the extension of technical education and those who seek to uphold
a " cultural " or " humanistic " ideal. This
friction is inevitable under capitalist conditions; but the reason for it would disappear
under economic democracy. Many persons
are led to-day, as a rule rightly, to oppose
extensions of technical training which are
good in themselves because, first, technical
training is far too narrowly conceived as a
routine business, and, secondly, technical instruction is put forward as a substitute for
other forms of education. Under democratic
conditions, it would be recognised that technical instruction, rightly understood, can be
made a cultural influence equally with book
learning, and that the two are intimately in-
terwoven and complementary. There would
thus be not antagonism, but co-operation;
but clearly special methods would be required
for the control and organisation of technical
education, and the various Guilds, and also
the professional associations, would require to
be brought very closely into contact with it.
Workshop or practical training and institu-
tional training would be recognised as complementary, and Guilds and professional associations would play a large part in the actual
control and administration of both. There is
no reason in this case for uniformity of system,
and probably many different systems would

8

prevail side by side, the common principle in all being the close joint action of the Education Guild with the other bodies concerned.

I am not suggesting, then, that technical education should fall outside the scope of the Education Guild; for that would hopelessly divide two forms of education which it is socially necessary to bind closely together. Special provision should be made within the Guild for the control of the technical side of education, and for the representation of industrial and professional interests in dealing with it. Thus, in Universities possessing a collegiate system, there might be included Colleges directly controlled, in large measure, by other Guilds or professional associations, but entering into the general work of the University, and submitting to its general regulation.

We have, then, Guilds for Education, Drama, Medicine, Sanitary (or Public Health) Services, and other civic services. But what, it will be asked, becomes of the "independent professions," scientific, statistical, artistic? What is to be the organisation and social status of the professional man for whom we have not indicated a place, and of the artist? I propose to say little on this point, beyond indicating that Guild Socialism is not intended to provide an answer to every question, or to provide a direct means of organising everybody in every one of his functional capacities.

Heaven forbid that we should be tidily organised down to the last man and the last function! Many functions and some men are mercifully unorganisable altogether, and many more can only be organised in small units constantly forming and dissolving with spontaneous bursts of co-operation and dissociation. But the forms of such co-operation, and the readiness with which such men and functions find the way to harmonious social organisation, depend essentially on the texture and spirit of the Society which surrounds them. In a community permeated, as the Guild community would be, by the associative impulse, scientific and professional association of all types would flourish exceedingly and secure readily the fullest social recognition, and, even the artists, least organisable of men, would respond to the associative impulses around them, and readily form co-operative groups, less stable, no doubt, but more vital by reason of their very instability. The professional associations of all types would, as we have seen again and again already, find most important functions to perform in the Guild community, and I think it is safe to say that nowhere would art and science flourish better, more widely, and more on a really popular basis, than in the diversely organised functional Society which I have described. For democracy in industry and in every sphere of social life has for its supreme justification its power to call out in the mass of men the creative, scientific and artistic impulses which capitalism suppresses or perverts, and to enable the now stifled civic spirit to work wonders in the regeneration of human taste and appreciation of the good things of life.

CHAPTER VII

THE STRUCTURE OF THE COMMUNE

WITH two important exceptions, we have now displayed in turn the principal forms of the functional organisation of Society, in so far as they enter into its economic or civic expression. The first exception, which we have made advisedly throughout this book, is the organisation of religion. It is significant that the recent development of theory concerning the relations of Church and State and the position of Churches in the modern community is running very largely on lines parallel to those of Guild development in the spheres of industry and civic service.[1] The essence, however, of the spiritual freedom of Churches, and indeed of all associations based on belief or opinion, lies in independence of the material

---

[1] See especially the writings of the late J. N. Figgis, and above all his *Churches in the Modern State.* See also Richard Roberts, *The Church in the Commonwealth.* There is also much that is closely relevant in the Report of the Archbishops' Committee on Church and State, and in the recent Church Enabling Act.

and economic, and even of the civic, structure
of Society, and in the working out of their
own problems in terms of spiritual, and not of
economic or civic, power, and certainly without invoking the material coercions of Society.
I have dealt more fully with this question elsewhere :[2] but it falls outside the scope of this
book.

The second exception lies in the sphere of
economics. Although the Guild organisation
of agriculture, even if it can be devised, will
clearly present many features differing from
those of the Guild organisation of industry,
nothing has hitherto been said about it here.
It is dealt with in a later chapter; but in this
chapter I shall have to a small extent to
introduce by name the Agricultural Guild,
without at all explaining what it is. This
arrangement seemed, in the circumstances,
the most convenient, since the discussion of
agricultural organisation involved the prior
discussion of some of the questions with which
this chapter will deal.

We have so far passed in review four distinct forms of organisation, each of which has
subdivisions of its own. First, we reviewed
the *producers'* organisation of the economic
Guilds; then, the *consumers'* organisation of
the Co-operative Movement and the Collective
Utility Councils; then the *civic service* or-

---

[2] See my *Social Theory*, chapter XI.

ganisation of the Civic Guilds; and lastly, the civic, or *citizen* organisation of the Cultural and Health Councils. In addition, we have already discussed, in a number of different aspects, the probable interrelation and inter-action of the various groups, both internally and one with another, both nationally and locally. But what we have not yet done is to give any idea of the working of all the groups as parts of a single system, that is to say, of the *communal*, as distinct from the functional, organisation and working of Guild Society.

We have to see, not merely how producer and consumer would meet and co-operate, or how civic servant and citizen are to meet and co-operate, but also how the communal spirit of the whole Society can find expression, in so far as such expression can be found at all in any form of social organisation.

This leads us directly to a further considera-tion of the position of " the State "; for orthodox social theorists usually claim for " the State " the supreme task of expressing the spirit of the community, and the positive power of co-ordinating and directing the ac-tivities of all the various parts of the social structure. We have so far attacked the notion of universal State Sovereignty from two dis-tinct points of view, and have, I think, made large breaches in the theory, without as yet destroying it altogether. First, we criticised

the structure of the State from the point of
view of functional democracy, showing that
its undifferentiated representative theory un-
fitted it to be the expression of a democratic
spirit which ought to find utterance in every
separate aspect of social activity. By this
criticism we destroyed the idea of State "omni-
competence." Secondly, in dealing with Collectivist theories in the economic sphere, we
destroyed the idea that the State represents
the consumer, and so excluded it from functional participation in the control of industry
or service. Inferentially, this criticism applied
also to the civic services in relation to which
we showed that representation must equally
have a functional basis. We have thus, besides destroying the notion of State "omni-
competence," definitely excluded it from a
place in the control of economic and civic
services alike. We have not, however, as yet
overthrown the notion of State Sovereignty
in a form in which it has been re-stated with
the definite purpose of meeting these objections.[3]

This revised theory rejects State omnicom-
petence and agrees, at least in general terms,
to the exclusion of the State from the normal
working of all social functions; but it retains
in the background a State "whose function is
Sovereignty," that is, which has no other task

---

[3] For instance, in a series of articles in the *New Age* a few years
ago.

than that of co-ordinating the activities of the various functional bodies in Society. Now, it is, of course, perfectly clear that the functional democracy which we have been expounding requires and must have a clearly recognised co-ordinating agency, and there would be no objection to calling this agency " the State," if the name did not immediately suggest two entirely misleading ideas. The first is that this new body will be historically continuous with the present political machinery of Society : the second is that it will, to a great extent, reproduce its structure, especially in being based on direct, non-functional election. The co-ordinating body which is required cannot be, in any real sense, historically continuous with the present State, and it must not reproduce in any important respect the structure of the present State. That it will not inherit most of its functions we have seen already.

The new co-ordinating body will not be continuous with the present political machinery of Society for two good and sufficient reasons. The first, clearly laid down in modern Marxist teaching, and most clearly of all by Lenin,[4] is that the present political machine is definitely an organ of class domination, not merely because it has been perverted by the power of capitalists, but because it is based on

---

4 See his book, *The State and Revolution*.

coercion, and is primarily an instrument of
coercion. Its essential idea is that of an externally imposed " order," and its transformation into a form expressive of self-government and freedom is impossible. Agreement
with Lenin on this point does not involve
agreement with him on the necessity of re-
placing the capitalist State by a temporary
"proletarian State," equally based on coercion
—a point which is discussed later in connection
with the problem of transition—but it does
involve agreement that, in a truly Socialist
Society, there will be no room for any body
continuous with the present political machine.

In the second place, this machine, where it
has adapted itself to so-called " political democracy," is based essentially on the false
idea of representative government which assumes that one man can represent another,
not *ad hoc*, in relation to a particular purpose
or group of purposes, but absolutely. This
false notion of representation we have already
rejected in favour of the functional idea.

But it may be argued that the defence of
the State, in its new form, meets this argument; for the new " function of the State "
is simply co-ordination, and nothing else.
This contention, however, will not hold water;
for the co-ordination of functions is not, and
cannot be, itself a function. Either co-
ordination includes the functions which it co-

ordinates, in which case the whole of social
organisation comes again under the domination of the State, and the whole principle of
functional democracy is destroyed; or it ex-
cludes them, and in this case it clearly cannot
co-ordinate. In other words, the State
" representative " either controls the economic and civic spheres, or he does not: if he
does, the representatives in these spheres lose
their self-government; if he does not, he cannot regulate their mutual relationships.

This second argument against the historical
continuity of the new co-ordinating body with
the present political machine also serves to
demonstrate that it will not reproduce the
latter's essential structure. It could do this
only if it were based on the false theory of
undifferentiated representation.

We can, then, safely assume that not only
will the present political machine lose its
economic and civic functions to new bodies,
but that the task of co-ordinating these functions will also pass out of its hands. It will
thus, at the least, " wither away " to a very
considerable extent, and I have no hesitation
in saying that, in my belief, it will disappear
altogether, either after a frontal attack, or by
atrophy following upon dispossession of its
vital powers. Conceivably, some fragments
of it may linger as formal instruments of the
new Society, as the Privy Council and other
obsolete survivals, including the Crown, linger

to-day; but in any case it will be of no real importance.

We have, then, to seek a new form of co-ordinating body which will not be inconsistent with the functional democracy on which our whole system is based. This can be nothing other than a bringing together of the various functional bodies whose separate working we have already described. Co-ordination is in-evitably coercive unless it is self-co-ordination, and it must therefore be accomplished by the common action of the various bodies which require co-ordination.

This problem of co-ordination has two separate aspects. It is first a problem of co-ordinating the functional bodies of the various types into a single communal system, and it is secondly a problem of co-ordinating bodies operating over a smaller with bodies operating over a larger area. Both these problems have to be solved in the structure of the co-ordinating, or as I shall henceforward call it, the *communal*, organisation of Guild Socialist Society.

In order, for the first discussion, to reduce the problem to as simple elements as possible, let us take it in the form in which it presents itself in a single town—say Norwich. In Norwich there will be at least the following bodies possessing important social functions:

(a) A number of Industrial Guilds organis-ing and managing various industries and economic services united in a Guild Council of delegates or representatives drawn from these Guilds; (b) a Co-operative Council; (c) a Collective Utilities Council; (d) a number of Guilds organising and managing various civic services—Civic Guilds; (e) a Cultural Council; and (f) a Health Council.

All these, not necessarily in the same proportions, have clearly a right to be represented on the communal body, which I shall call hereafter simply the *Commune*. I have no desire to lay down in detail any definite numerical basis of representation; but the number of representatives from the Industrial Guilds, who might be chosen either by each Guild or through the Guild Council, would probably be approximately equal to the number from the Co-operative and Collective Utilities Councils taken together, and the number from the Civic Guilds to the number from the Cultural and Health Councils together. The proportion assigned to the economic and the non-economic groups would certainly vary from case to case.

The bodies so far mentioned, however, do not necessarily complete the composition of the Commune. In any instance, there might be special organisations to which it would be desirable, on account of their importance in the town, to give representation. Again, what is far more important, the town as a whole cannot be treated as an undifferentiated unit. In electing their representatives to serve on the four Councils mentioned above,[5] the citizens, if the town were of any size, would almost certainly vote by Wards and each member on a Council would sit there as a Ward representative in relation to his particular function. It is of the first importance, if this representation is to be a reality, that the Ward should exist, not merely as a polling district for various elections, but also as an active centre for the expression of local opinion, which requires, for its successful eliciting, to be made articulate within the smallest natural areas of common feeling. Indeed, in the sphere both of consumers' and of civic organisation, the Ward in the town and the village in the country form the natural equivalents for the workshop in the sphere of industry or the school in the sphere of education.

The Wards, then, in our case of Norwich, must have a real existence, and the Ward representatives must report back regularly to, and receive instructions and advice from, Ward Meetings of all the dwellers in the Ward who choose to attend. The Ward Meeting would also exercise, within the limits to be discussed hereafter, the right of recalling from any Council the Ward representative. It would also, especially in the larger towns, have as-

---

[5] I.e., Councils as distinct from Guilds, which would have their own varying electoral methods.

signed to it certain administrative functions which are best carried out over a very small area, and would execute these either in full Ward Meeting, or by the appointment of *ad hoc* and usually temporary committees or officers. Where, in a large centre, the functions of the Wards expanded, standing Ward Committees might be developed, and it might be desirable that these Ward Committees should have direct representation, in respect of their functions, on the Town Commune.[6] In such cases, these representatives would form a third group distinct both from the Guild and from the Council representatives.

Having laid down the essential structure of the Norwich Commune, let us try to see more explicitly what work it would have to do. What we say under this head will apply, with small changes, to the other types of Commune hereafter described. Clearly, it would be, in the main, not an administrative but a co-ordinating body. The various services would be managed by their Guilds and their policy would be determined by the co-operative working of the Guilds and the appropriate citizen Councils. Five essential tasks would remain for the Commune itself. First, it would have to agree upon the allocation of the

6 I assume that the election of the various Council representatives would be by ballot of the Wards, but that these Ward Committee representatives would be chosen either by the Ward Committee, or, better, from the Ward Committee by the Ward Meeting Uniformity, however, is not necessary.

local resources among the various services
calling for expenditure—that is, it would have
essential *financial* functions, and would be,
indeed, the financial pivot of the whole Guild
system in the area.   Secondly, it would be
the court of appeal in all cases of difference
between functional bodies of different types.
Thus, if the Co-operative Society could not
agree on some point of policy with the Guilds
operating in the sphere of " domestic " production and distribution, the Commune would
have to hear the case and give its judgment.
Thirdly, it would determine the lines of demarcation between the various functional
bodies, where any question concerning them
arose.'   Fourthly, it would itself take the
initiative in any matter concerning the town
as a whole and not in any functional capacity,
such as a proposed extension of town boundaries or a proposal to build a new town hall.
The original suggestion, in such cases, would
probably come from one of the functional
bodies or from a Ward; but they would be
matters for the Town Commune itself to decide.   Fifthly, so far as coercive machinery,
such as a police force, remained, it should be
controlled, not by any single functional body,
but by all jointly—that is by the Commune.
This, as we shall see, applies also in the realm

7 I do not mean, of course, that if two Industrial Guilds fell out, the
Commune would settle the matter. It would go to the Guild Council.
But if the Guild Council failed to settle it, even such a difference might
go to the Commune.

of law.[8] The Commune could decide to hand over, and would, wherever possible, be wise to hand over actual administrative functions falling within its sphere to the Wards, in order to preserve the most direct form of popular control. Thus, I should like to see the Wards appoint and control the police—a reversion to the days of the town or village constable.

Before we attempt to examine these functions in greater detail, let us complete our survey of the communal structure by applying to other areas the principles which we have just illustrated in the case of the town. First, let us see in very general terms what would be the corresponding forms of organisation in the countryside. Corresponding to the Ward, but needing larger powers of administration in accordance with its more self-contained character, is the Village, which would have its Village Meeting and, in most cases, its Village Committee. No elaborate representative forms would be required, as to a great extent all the citizens could manage their affairs directly.

In addition to serving as the smallest administrative unit in the countryside, the village would be the electoral unit for the organisation of the next stage of rural government. This I call the "Township," in order to emphasise its correspondence to the

[8] See page 49ff.

" Town " stage of urban organisation. It is a group of villages or small towns, probably varying greatly in size from place to place, but always larger than the present Parish and smaller than most of the existing Administrative Counties. It would not include the larger Towns falling within its area,[9] and would thus be mainly rural and agricultural. Here again, there would be a Commune—this time a *Township Commune*, and the basis of representation would be largely the same as in the Town. Apart from the fact that the Village would replace the Ward, the various groups—Industrial Guilds, Civic Guilds, Co-operative Society, Collective Utilities Council, Cultural Council, Health Council—would usually recur, though their relative importance might be different, and would be represented on the Township Commune. But side by side with them would be another organisation of the greatest rural importance—the Agricultural Guild. Of this body, which is described later in this book, I need say no more now than that it would probably combine, for the agricultural population, the functions of a Guild as a producers' organisation with those of an agricultural Co-operative Society. It would be directly and strongly represented on the Township Commune.

---

[9] I assume that most " Urban Districts " of to-day would be recognised as Towns. Smaller semi-urban centres would count as villages and would be included in the " Township."

When we proceed to consider larger areas of administration, new problems at once arise. One cardinal defect of our present system of local government is that, recognising no area larger than the administrative county and smaller than the nation, it is incapable of securing effective administration of services, such as electricity and road transport, which require common action over a considerable area, or of co-ordinating town and countryside into a single administrative system. These needs can be met only by the method of regional organisation, and, without developing the full case for regionalism here, I propose to assume that Guild Society will adopt, in response to an evident need, a regional basis of organisation.[10] I must, however, in order that the exposition here given may be intelligible, state very briefly what I understand by a " Region."

I believe that England, for example, falls naturally into a number of areas which are at once centres of economic life, of common social outlook, and of common administrative problems. These Regions are not equal in size, in population, or in wealth, but none, with the possible exception of the London area—Cobbett's " Wen "—is too large for reasonable balance or too small for effective

10 The case for regionalism is briefly stated in my *Social Theory*, chapter X, and I am developing it fully in relation to the Guild idea, in a forthcoming book, *The Reorganisation of Local Government*.

administration of the services which exceed the capacity of the present local authorities. As instances, I will only give the following :—

(1) The North-East (Northumberland, Durham and the Cleveland district of Yorkshire). (2) The West Riding of Yorkshire (except the Sheffield area, which falls into a separate group) with the North Riding (except Cleveland), and the East Riding. (3) Devonshire and Cornwall. (4) The Eastern Counties. (5) The South-West (Gloucester, Somerset, Hereford, Wiltshire).

These are only approximate examples, given to illustrate the general case. I do not say that the regional boundary would always follow exactly county boundaries, though it would be convenient for it to do so as far as possible.[11]

Each Region would be a complex of town and country, and the Regional Commune would have to be based on a full recognition of this fact. It would, of course, have to provide in the first place for the direct representation of the various functional bodies within the Region. The form of this representation is clear enough on the Guild side; for the Guilds, industrial, agricultural, or civic, would have their own regional administrations, and

[11] For a detailed exposition, with which I am largely, though not completely in agreement, see Mr. C. D. Fawcett's excellent book, *The Provinces of England*.

from these the Guild representatives would be drawn. But we have so far said nothing of regional organisation of consumers or of citizens, which is clearly required to correspond to the regional Guilds and to express the consumers' or the civic point of view in relation to the regional services.

Clearly, then, there must be regional Co-operative Societies or Unions, regional Collective Utilities Councils, and regional Cultural Councils and Health Councils. These, I believe, would be best constituted of representatives from the various local functional Councils of the Towns and Townships within the Region. This, it is true, involves indirect election, to which many professing democrats take objection; but I have no faith at all in the virtues of direct election except when it can be combined with a constant touch of the body of voters with their representative. Thus, direct election is good in the Village or the Ward, because all the electors can meet with, question, and instruct their representative face to face; but it is a farce in the case of Parliament, where the constituency is too large for the elected person to preserve any real contact with those who elected him. The real safeguard for the voter is to preserve the fullest form of democracy, including the right of recall, in the small units within which real contact is possible, and to rely on this contact and power of recall for the carrying out of the popular will in the larger bodies. These larger bodies can themselves best be composed of delegates from the bodies working within the smaller areas, always provided that these delegates themselves preserve constant contact with the smaller bodies which choose them, and are subject to the right of these bodies to recall them at any time.

It is curious that those persons who profess to be most solicitous for "democracy," and are therefore most vehement against indirect election, are often equally firm in their opposition to the recall. To me it seems that, with the recall in operation as an absolutely vital democratic safeguard, the question of direct or indirect election reduces itself largely to one of convenience, whereas without the recall I admit the vice of indirect election. It is therefore essential to state clearly what, in this connection, the recall involves; for, if A is elected by a Ward to represent it on the Norwich Health Council and is sent by that body to represent it on the East Anglian Regional Health Council, the question at once arises which body has the right to recall A if it disapproves of his doings. It seems clear that the Norwich Council has the right to recall him from the Regional Council; but has the Ward, by recalling him from the Norwich Council, the right indirectly to recall him from the Regional Council also? I should say not; for on the Regional Council he was representing, not the Ward, but Norwich. What might best happen would seem to be this. As soon as A is chosen by the Norwich Health Council to serve on the Regional Council, the Ward he represents should be entitled to elect a substitute representative to serve as long as he was engaged upon the higher service. This representative would be subject to recall by the Ward; but A could be recalled only by the Norwich Health Council. When, however, the period for which he was elected by the Ward expired, he would have to come back to the Ward for re-election before he could become eligible for reappointment on the Regional Council. Is not this a fair and workable solution of the difficulty?

We have, then, already in mind the composition of the Regional Commune. It repeats in its essential features, the structure of the smaller Communes already described; but it differs from them in bringing together town and country. Instead, therefore, of representatives from Wards or Villages, the representatives of the smaller local bodies within it are drawn from the Town and Township Communes. We thus get, side by side with representatives of the smaller urban and rural area administrations within it, the representatives of the Guilds, Industrial, Agricultural and Civic, of the consumers' organisations, Co-operative and Collective, of the Cultural and Health Councils, and perhaps of one or

two other bodies of special importance in the
life of the Region.

According to our current terminology, all
the foregoing Communes would be regarded
as organs of Local Government. At present,
however, we draw a sharp and almost absolute
distinction between Local and Central Government. In the decentralised Guild Society of
which we are speaking, no such sharp distinction would exist; for by far the greatest part
of the work of the community would be carried on and administered locally or regionally,
and the central work would be divided, according to function, among a considerable
number of distinct organisations. There
would therefore be neither need nor opportunity for a centre round which a vast aggre-
gation of bureaucratic and coercive machinery
could grow up. The national co-ordinating
machinery of Guild Society would be essentially unlike the present State, and would have
few direct administrative functions. It would
be mainly a source of a few fundamental decisions on policy, demarcation between functional bodies, and similar issues, and of final
adjudications on appeals in cases of dispute;
but it would not possess any vast machinery
of its own, save that, as long as military and
naval force continued to be employed, it would
have to exercise directly the control of such
force, as it would indirectly and in the last
resort of the law. Foreign relations, so far

as they did not deal exclusively with matters falling within the sphere either of the economic or of the civic bodies, would fall to its lot; but the victory of democracy in other communities would tend to reduce these non-functional external activities to a minimum.[12] The existence, which we have already assumed, of national functional organisations, based on the local and regional bodies, in all the various spheres of social action, would functionalise national equally with local and regional activities.

Into the National Commune, then, would enter the representatives of the National Guilds, Agricultural, Industrial and Civic, of the National Councils economic and civic, and of the Regional Communes themselves. Its general structure would thus be essentially the same as that of the smaller Communes which, equally with the national functional bodies, it would exist to co-ordinate. It would be a much less imposing body as the central organ of Society than the Great Leviathan of to-day, with its huge machinery of coercion and bureaucratic government. But it would be none the worse for that; for where the spirit of community is most at home, there is the machinery of central government likely to be least in evidence.

I recognise fully that the foregoing descrip-

12 For a further treatment of this question, see the concluding Chapter.

tion may seem a very formal and dogmatic account and far too tidy to be true. I fully admit it. It is a typical and not an actual structure that I am describing, and in practice, even if the Guild system came to be fully adopted, there would obviously be all sorts of divergences from the theoretical type. It is, however, necessary, in order to be able to argue clearly about the way in which the Guild system would actually work, to lay down its essential structure with a somewhat disagreeable amount of precision. This does no harm, and helps argument very greatly, as long as those who use this method realise that the structure which they are imagining is typical only, and can never become actual in the precise form in which they imagine it. Human institutions do not develop in exact accordance with logical rules, and, while their essential development may be guided by human wills, the exact form of social changes is largely determined by historical accidents. So it will be even if Guildsmen get their way entirely; and it is, of course, far more likely that the coming Society will be a resultant of different influences, and will incorporate in its structure no theoretical system as a whole, but parts of many and conflicting systems. Nor need we wish it otherwise.

CHAPTER VIII

THE WORKING OF THE COMMUNE

Our last chapter, with a compression dictated by considerations of space, described the communal structure of Guild Socialist Society, local, regional and national. We have now to make the attempt to show this Society in action, and to face the question of its manner of dealing with certain of the fundamental problems of social relationships. We described the main functions of the various Communes as falling under five heads, and we shall probably do best to follow in our treatment of problems the arrangement which we there employed.

We have, then, to deal with the working of communal Society under a Guild system in relation to the five following groups of problems :—

(a) financial problems, especially the allocation of national resources, provision of capital, and, to a certain extent, regulation of incomes and prices;

(b) differences arising between functional bodies on questions of policy;

(c) constitutional questions of demarcation between functional bodies;

(d) questions not falling within the sphere of any functional authority, including general questions of external relations;

(e) coercive functions.

These five groups fall, in the main, under two larger groupings. The first three are all questions of co-ordination in the narrower sense, while the two last are questions, not themselves of a co-ordinating character, which necessarily fall to the body which exercises the task of co-ordination.

In considering the first three groups, we must bear in mind throughout that all the various functions whose working they co-ordinate are fully exercised by various functional bodies working in close and constant co-operation under conditions which we have already laid down. They do not give rise, therefore, to important administrative acts of the Commune itself, which passes on its decisions for execution by these functional bodies. I can simply illustrate what I mean by saying that the present amorphous and swollen Civil Service, so far as its work continues at all, will not for the most part continue to act as the direct servant of the Commune, but will be distributed among the various Guilds and Councils. This will be the case with the Local Government service as well, and indeed almost the whole administrative mechanism of the present day will be broken up and re-organised in connection with the various functional associations. Each of these, as well as the Communes themselves, will require a small " Civil Service " of its own, just as a Trade Union or an Employers' Association to-day has its staff of administrators and clerks. The number of these, relatively to the producing section of the people, will, however, be immensely reduced by the abolition of capitalism; for it is private property that is mainly responsible for the inflation of non-productive labour.

We can best approach our first group of problems by considering first the case of any single commodity, and proceeding from that to the more complicated questions involved. The Distributive Guild distributes milk, let us suppose, which it gets from the Agricultural Guild. The Co-operative Society has the task of dealing with the milk question from the consumers' standpoint. Let us confine our attention for the present to the price at which the milk is sold, without raising other questions which may arise. How is this price determined? Presumably, the Distributive Guild, basing its estimate on the price it pays to the

Agricultural Guild, and on its own cost of distribution, proposes a price, which it submits to the Co-operative Society. If the two agree, the agreed price becomes the actual selling price without further question. If they disagree, the question must go to the Commune (local, regional or national, as the case may be) for discussion and final decision. But probably before a final disagreement is reached, a good many considerations emerge. If the Co-operative Society is satisfied that the distributive cost allowed for by the Distributive Guild is reasonable, but thinks that the price paid to the Agricultural Guild is too high, it can either alone, or jointly with the Distributive Guild, take the matter up with the Agricultural Guild directly, and again, failing agreement, carry the matter to the Commune. The Distributive Guild, again, can by itself take up the question with the Agricultural Guild; but in this case the question, being one between two Guilds, would, if the Agricultural Guild belonged to the Industrial Guilds Congress, go to that body rather than to the Commune. In one or another of these ways, a price for milk satisfactory to the social sense of the community —in other words, a " Just Price "—would be arrived at. This, we may assume, would be the normal method of determining prices in a Guild Society.

There is, however, a further social consideration which might arise. It might be considered desirable, for social reasons, to sell a particular commodity at either more or less than the natural price based on its cost of production. Any such decision would have to go before the Commune, which would determine the allocation of any surplus so realised, or the method of bearing any loss. This is, in fact, Guild " excise " and its opposite.

This consideration of the question of prices, however, only leads on to a much bigger problem—that of " capital." One of the most frequent questions asked of Guild Socialists is how industry and services generally would be financed under a Guild Society; for clearly it would not be by the present methods, ranging from real " saving " out of income to capitalist credit manufacture by financial interests. The understanding of this point depends on a clear appreciation of the fact that all real additions to capital take the form of directing a part of the productive power of labour and using certain materials not for the manufacture of ultimate products or the rendering of ultimate services but to the manufacture of products and the rendering of services incidental to such manufacture for purposes of further production. If I spend a thousand pounds on suppers at the Savoy, I consume the product of so much labour : if I spend the same amount on causing a workshop to be equipped with necessary new plant, I add so much to the " capital " available for future production.

It is far from being the case that the larger the proportion of its labour power a community allocates to " capital " production the happier its members are : but it is essential at all times, and in accordance with considerations which vary from time to time, for a community to preserve a balance between production for ultimate use and production for use in further production. And this balance is a matter which ought to be determined by and on behalf of the whole community, in all its various aspects and functions.   It is not a matter purely for the economic organisations of producers and con-sumers—for economic Guilds and consumers' Councils—since it concerns just as vitally the civic organisations.   If more is spent on economic services there will be less to spend on education, which needs both incomes for its teachers and labour for buildings, books and equipment of all sorts.

The allocation, therefore, of the communal productive resources is a matter for the Com-mune as a whole, and the Commune, either locally, regionally, or nationally, as the case may be, will have to decide both on the alloca-tions to be made to " consumable " and to " capital " production and to the services of a non-economic character, and, in detail, on the allocation to be made to each industry or ser-vice.   Whether this is expressed in terms of money or not does not matter : it is essentially an allocation of material and labour, and fundamentally, an allocation of human productive power.

What, then, will be the method by which the Commune will arrive at this allocation? Normally each Guild, economic or civic, will prepare a budget, showing its estimate of requirements both of goods or services for immediate use, and of extensions and improvements. In the preparation of these budgets, the Guilds will clearly consult one another. These Guild budgets will go before the various Councils of consumers or citizens, and the Councils will be able either to criticise and secure amendment, or to put in alternative requisitions of their own. In any case, all the budgets, with all proposed amendments and requisitions, will go before the Commune, or probably in the first instance before its Finance Committee, which will have its staff of expert statisticians. The various budgets will there be brought into harmony with the estimated national production, and, after any necessary further negotiations have taken place, the complete budget will come up before the Commune as a whole for ratification. In it will be included the estimated administrative and other charges of the Commune itself, which will be levied directly on the Guilds as a form of taxation at source.

Thus, the allocation of the communal labour-power and the provision of capital will become matters directly regulated by the Commune,

and will not be left, as they are now, to the
blind play of economic forces or the machina-
tions of financiers.   There will be, for the first
time, an ordered balance of "saving and
spending," and a reasoned allocation of effort
to various services in accordance with their respective degrees of social utility.   And all this
will be done by the method of real self-government, each service and interest having a full
opportunity of putting its point of view, and
taking part in the communal decision.   Moreover, this will take place locally and regionally,
in respect of local and regional services, as well
as nationally.

The Guild budgets will, of course, as we saw
in an earlier chapter,[1] include their estimates of
salaries to be paid to their members, and all
questions of income will thus come within the
sphere of the Commune for effective criticism.
Moreover, the Commune will itself have the
task of determining the allocation of income to
those sections of the people who are not
in receipt of an income directly from a functional body.   All forms of provision at the communal expense, whether by direct grant of
income or not, would be determined by the
Commune.

The Guild system has thus a perfectly easy
and flexible instrument of taxation.   It does
not tax the individual, save perhaps in excep-

1 See page 72.

tional cases, such as enterprises continuing to be conducted outside the Guild system. It taxes at source and draws the sums approved by the Commune in the form of an agreed claim on the labour-power of the Guilds. Moreover, the distributions of the Guilds in the form of income to their members and also their allocations to capital account being regulated by the Commune, any surplus realised by a Guild in its annual working would pass to the Commune for allocation, or be set off against the claim of communal services on the productive Guilds as a whole.

Let me again emphasise the fact that, in practice, the greater part of all this detailed financial work would not be done by the Commune at all, but directly and in consultation by the various functional bodies. Only moot points needing settlement and general questions of principle would normally come before the Commune.

Before we leave the question of finance, it is necessary to add that, whether the Guilds or the Guild Congress maintain their own Banks or not, it follows from what has been said that the issue of credit would be controlled by the Commune, and that the Guilds could only work within the limits authorised by it. Otherwise, the balance between " saving " and " spending," and among the various services, would at once break down, and the door be again opened to inflation and deflation in new

forms.   The Commune would clearly control
the currency, and the general banking system
would also be communal.

This brings us to our second group of
problems—those dealing with the determination of differences arising on questions of policy
between functional bodies.   This need not
detain us long; for the procedure would be
essentially the same as that which has been
already described in' the case of differences concerning prices or cost of production.   There
would first be every possible effort to arrive at
agreement by the method of direct negotiation
between the bodies concerned, and a question
would only come to the Commune, local,
regional or national, after all efforts to agree
upon it directly had failed.   Moreover, a question arising between two bodies of the same
type—between two Guilds, for example—
would nominally be dealt with, on the failure
of the bodies concerned to reach an agreement,
not by the Commune, but by the larger body
including both the organisations concerned—
the Guild Council or Congress, in this case.
The Communes would thus have to deal, in
this sphere, only with exceptional cases.   This
they would probably do, as a rule, through
special committees assisted by experts; for it
is probable that most of the detailed work of the
Commune would be done through committees
similar to those which now exist in local
authorities, and whose adoption by Parliament

Mr. F. W. Jowett has long been unsuccessfully, but very reasonably, urging.

The third group of questions—constitutional issues of demarcation and powers arising between functional bodies—although they are to some extent similar to policy issues—raises far more fundamental considerations; for they involve the whole problem of constitutional law under a functionally organised Society. It is clear that the body which would pass constitutional laws determining the respective spheres of the various functional bodies would be the Commune. Some such laws would, no doubt, be regional and local; but we may take the National Commune as the typical body concerned in this task. The laws, then, are passed by the National Commune, not necessarily, though possibly, in the shape of a formal written constitution; and clearly the National Commune is also the body which has power to alter the laws. It is the Constituent Assembly and the constitutional legislature of Guild democracy.

Disputes, however, will inevitably arise as to the meaning and interpretation of these laws in particular cases, both on broad general questions of powers and functions, and on quite minor points. These will clearly have to be dealt with by means of a judicial system, and it seems evident that the judicial system must be directly subordinate to the Commune. The legal profession would have its Guild and its strongly developed internal self-government; but judges would be appointed, from the qualified members of the profession, by the Commune. These judges would deal with ordinary constitutional cases; but the National Commune should have the power, not merely of passing laws, but, in any disputed case of interpretation, of declaring its interpretation of the law, which should be binding upon the judges. This task would fall most naturally to a special Constitutional Committee of the National Commune, whose decisions would require ratification by the National Commune itself.

I am here speaking directly, not of the whole body of law, but of the law relating to constitutional questions. It seems clear, however, that the legal and judicial system as a whole would be organised according to the same principles of internal self-government for the legal profession, the appointment of judges by the Communes, nationally or regionally, and the enforcement by the judges of the communal law. In a sense, the Guilds and other functional bodies would also legislate, as local authorities do now by means of bye-laws; but they could do so only within the powers conferred by the communal constitution, and any law of a functional body involving coercion should, I think, only become enforceable in the communal courts after ratification by the Commune, except in so far as the coercive power was definitely assigned to the functional body under a constitutional law of the Commune. The operation side by side of a number of distinct judicial systems would create an impossible situation, and the judicial system must therefore be one, and form a part of the structure of the Commune itself.

What I have said of judges and the Legal Guild applies only to the higher courts. In courts of " summary jurisdiction," I should, in a democratic Society not troubled by class differences, favour the continuance of lay justices of the peace, nominated by the local Communes. There should also be a right of any layman to plead in such courts, and in them legal formalities should be kept down to the minimum. This would not lead, in a Society not burdened with social classes or capitalistic disputes about property, to the confusion which it might involve at the present day.

Our fourth group of questions carries us into quite a different sphere; for we are now concerned, not with the co-ordinating work of the Communes, but with the positive tasks belonging to them and not falling within the sphere of any functional body. These tasks are of three kinds. First, there are tasks which, by reason of their nature, must be retained in the hands of the body which exercises the task of co-ordination. Clearly, as long as the possibility of war remains, the power of declaring war and peace must belong to the Commune, and this in turn involves direct control of armed forces, as long as they remain.   Army and Navy would, no doubt, be internally organised on Guild lines, and we may hope that the Army at least would be, not a standing full-time force, but a voluntary part-time Army of citizens pursuing normally other avocations. Such an Army could be, to a great extent, administered by the local and regional Communes, and would certainly not be likely to demonstrate any acute desire to go to war.   A full discussion of this question, however, would carry us much too far afield.

The assigning to the Communes of the power of war and peace does not, of course, mean that the whole of foreign relations would fall within their sphere.   The whole work of foreign trade and commercial relations, for example, would be administered by the Guilds, working in conjunction with the economic Councils of consumers.   International civic relations, again, would fall within the sphere of the civic Guilds and Councils.   It is, however, clear that, on a difference of view among the functional bodies concerned, any matter of international economic or civic policy might be referred to the Commune, and questions of mixed economic or cultural and political relationships would be normally so referred.   The National Commune would thus be the supreme representative of the nation abroad ; but its organisation would ensure that the economic and civic bodies had their proper places in Embassies and Legations, while the consular service would probably become either a Guild service, or one very closely linked up with the Guilds. A particular Guild, too, would doubtless often maintain its own representatives and trading stations abroad.

The second kind of task belonging to our fourth group has to do with questions which concern either the area of the community as a whole or the distribution of areas within it. The main examples of this type are territorial questions of boundaries and colonial possessions, while they continue to exist, and similar questions of boundaries and extensions in the case of Regions, Towns and Townships. These are clearly matters which concern the community as a whole and each of the functional bodies severally. The Commune is therefore the natural body to deal with them.

The third task falling within the fourth group raises more difficult questions. However fully the functional organisation of Society is developed, there will remain matters which neither fall readily within the sphere of any of the functional bodies, nor call for the creation of a separate functional organisation to deal with them. These the Communes would either assign to the functional body best able to undertake them, or, if this could not be done, would themselves undertake and administer. It would, of course, always be possible, if at any

stage the creation of a separate functional body
for a particular purpose became desirable, for
the Communes to call such a body into
existence, either nationally or in a smaller
area; and probably the method by which the
Communes would administer such services
would be by the creation of special committees
or forms of organisation on which the various
points of view concerned would be represented.   These would serve as a nucleus if, at
a later stage, it became necessary to create a
complete functional organisation.

It is difficult to give actual instances of the
type of question here contemplated; for the
provision is intended mainly to meet conditions which can hardly be foreseen.   There is,
however, one sphere of social life to which this
proposal has a special relevance.   In these
proposals for the communal structure of Guild
Society no provision is made for a special body
to deal with the whole sphere of personal and
private relationships—questions of personal
conduct and of personal property relations.
This is largely because I believe that these
matters should be as little regulated as
possible, except by the force of opinion, and
that the need for laws affecting them would
be greatly reduced in a democratic Society.
They would, however, clearly remain and have
to be regulated to some extent.   Either
separate bodies could be created in Towns,
Townships and Regions, and in the Nation as

a whole, on the same basis as the various functional Councils of consumers and citizens, or the work of regulation could be undertaken, better as I believe, by the Communes themselves, acting through special committees appointed for the purpose and including representatives both from the various functional associations and from various forms of voluntary association existing in the community. It is even possible that the parliamentary machine, shorn of its economic and civic functions, might be adapted to deal with this matter, by the survival of this particular group of functions in its hands. Control by the Commune would, however, be likely to keep down to the minimum the amount of social interference in private concerns; and for this reason there is something to be said in its favour. In any case, laws affecting personal relationships and conduct, and involving coercion, would require, like other coercive laws, ratification by the Commune.

The fifth and last group of questions with which we set ourselves to deal in this chapter is in reality less a separate group than a problem arising in relation to all the others. It is therefore natural that it has been touched on to a considerable extent already. The coercive power of the Communes involves two separate sets of considerations, the coercion of individuals into conformity with the communal law, and the coercion of functional bodies.   Coercion is a bad thing, and that Society is best which, being founded on just social arrangements, can dispense with it to the fullest extent.   Nevertheless, any Society has at present to provide for it and to have a means of invoking it in the last resort.   In relation to the individual, the difficulty is not to provide Society with the means of coercion, but to prevent it from employing the means it possesses far too stringently and often.   Protection against this would be afforded, under Guild Socialist conditions, first by the fact that the central government would be comparatively on a small scale and would thus not have in a high degree the tendency to usurp and absorb authority, and secondly by the prevalence of association in many forms, which would afford to the individual a valuable protection which he now often lacks in face of the " Great Leviathan."

This, however, only brings us to the second problem, that of the coercion of a group, such as a Guild, which might refuse to abide by the communal decision.   It is clear that direct coercion of such a group by means of an economic boycott, if the social opinion of the community were aroused, would be possible, but extremely undesirable.   It is, however, necessary to point out that this difficulty can be raised in very much the same way whatever the social system may be; for we do not find it easy to coerce large and powerful groups to-day, although the State is nominally and theoretically equipped with full authority to do so.

The point of view from which this question ought primarily to be regarded is not really that of coercion at all. Coercion of a powerful group is inevitably not far removed from civil war, if the will to resist is present in the group; and Society ought therefore to be so ordered that such coercion shall be only invoked in the last resort, and shall be scarcely ever, if at all, required. The best way of making this provision is by ensuring for every reasonable claim the fullest possible amount of social consideration; for this will have the effect, not only in most cases of destroying the will of the group to resist a communal decision, but of bringing the social opinion of the community, which is a far more effective instrument than direct coercion, actively to bear upon the group. Guild Society is built on the basis of trusting the people, and of placing power, and with it responsibility, in the hands of the functional bodies. This means that these bodies, with the fullest chances of stating their case before the Commune, will be most unlikely to resist a communal decision if it goes against them. Our experience of present conditions ought to have taught us the futility of endeavouring to coerce men into a mood of service plainly enough to persuade us that the better way is that of trusting them. Trust does not and cannot involve the abandonment of all powers of coercion in the last resort; but it does involve that reliance should be placed mainly on the pressure of argument and communal opinion.   We want to build a new Society which will be conceived in the spirit, not of coercion, but of free service, and in the belief, not that men must be driven, but that they are capable of leading themselves, if the conditions of democratic fellowship are assured.   That is the spirit in which we must work, regarding the coercion of either group or individual as a last and desperate remedy, and seeing in the functional organisation of Society an immense inspiration to willing service and an indispensable safeguard of personal liberty.

I am fully conscious that this description of the communal working of Guild Society is in many respects inadequate, and in others far too dogmatic.   It is, however, as many writers of Utopias have found, difficult to put life into an account of the working of a theoretical system except by sacrificing the accuracy of the picture.   The most valuable part of the life and spirit of a community is nearly always that which most escapes from formal organisation.   Any picture, therefore, of the working of social organisation is far indeed from being a picture of the real life of the community; and this is even more true of a really democratic Society than under existing conditions. For the effect of real democracy will be an immense liberation of social and individual energy; and this will flow, not only or mainly into the communal organisation of Society, but into all its voluntary and informal associations, and most of all into the personal relationships and activities of its members. This unorganised spirit of the people does not escape the historian who knows his business, though it is difficult enough to recapture; but the theorist who sets out to plan a social system for the future cannot call up this spirit, although he knows that his work, because of its absence, runs a big risk of seeming unreal and out of touch with the deepest human needs. But it is not because they worship organisation for its own sake that Guildsmen build their plans for a new social structure: it is because they believe that this structure will liberate energy and promote happiness and achievement in countless directions which it is impossible to foresee.

I am conscious also that the impression conveyed by this book, and especially by this chapter and the last, may be that of a terrible and bewildering complexity of social organisation in which the individual will be lost. I ask anyone who is inclined to hold that view to devote a brief period to studying the social organisation of to-day, not merely in its parliamentary and political forms, but with all its complexity of capitalist, labour, professional, cultural, and other forms of association. Let him then ask himself which is the more complicated, and whether it is not the case that the conditions of to-day result everywhere in a medley of conflicting and warring associations formed, for the most part, in order not to fulfil a social function, but to get the best one of another. He will find the structure which I have described both far less complicated and far better adapted to its purpose than the structure of existing capitalist Society.

CHAPTER IX

GUILD SOCIALISM IN AGRICULTURE

SOCIALIST theories have almost always been based mainly on urban experience, and have found the main body of their adherents among the town workers of the industrial system. Agricultural labourers have, indeed, from time to time organised, usually for a brief period, on Trade Union lines, and various forms of Co-operation, more or less democratic in character, have in many countries struck firm roots in the agricultural population; but Socialists applying themselves to rural problems have usually breathed in the manner of fish out of water. It is true that there has been at all times among Socialists a marked tendency to hold strong opinions about the land, and to stress the iniquity of the private absorption of rent. It is true also that, on more than one occasion a strong " back to the land " enthusiasm has developed in the urban working-class movement, as in the " Land

Scheme " of Feargus O'Connor and the Owenite ideal of Co-operative settlements in the early nineteenth century, and in Blatchford's *Merrie England* and the writings of Kropotkin in more recent times.   But probably no Socialist Party except the Social Revolutionaries of Russia had until the last few years any considerable agrarian following ; and, even to-day, nearly all the Socialist and Labour Parties, to say nothing of the rural Trade Unions themselves, are without a clear, practical and constructive policy capable of being applied to agricultural production.

That this is a fact and a serious weakness is generally recognised, both in the countries in which peasant ownership largely prevails and in those which, like Great Britain, possess a large farmer class and a corresponding agricultural proletariat.   To these two types of countries the problem clearly presents to a large extent a different aspect, at least when immediate policy is in question.   It may also well be that the wide differences which now exist in methods of agricultural production under capitalism will persist under Socialist conditions, although they will greatly change their character.

Have Guildsmen a way of dealing with the agricultural problem, or, in other words, does the Guild philosophy which I have been expounding convey any clear message as to the best form of agricultural organisation in a free Society? Clearly, the problem is one which will have to be worked out in the main by agriculturalists themselves; and I shall only attempt in this chapter to give a very general indication of the way in which a " layman " looks at it in the light of the general Guild principles that have been already stated. Nor shall I attempt to deal at all with the wider question of the relative places which industrial and agricultural production should occupy in a healthy community, not because it is not important, but because it would take me much too far afield.[1]

It is clear at the outset that our general principles prescribe two things—first that the workers on the land, under whatever systems they work, must enjoy forms of self-government corresponding to those of industrial, professional and civic service workers; and secondly that the private appropriation of rent must give way to a communal appropriation. But our principles do not prescribe either large-scale cultivation or small-scale cultivation, either the elimination or the continuance of the peasant form of individual farming. A good many Socialists, especially of the " State Socialist " variety, have fallen into the error of assuming that Socialism commits them to

[1] As I write, the National Guilds League, with the aid of its members who have a practical agricultural experience, is endeavouring to work out its answer to this problem. What I say in this chapter is purely a personal and provisional opinion, which I am quite ready to change, on reason shown.

large-scale State farming, and that agriculture
cannot be ripe for Socialism until capitalist
methods have been applied to it, and small-
scale cultivation either eliminated or greatly
reduced.   Kautsky, for instance, argues on
these lines in his attack on Bolshevism, and the
Bolshevists, while they are realists enough not
to attempt to force " communist " agriculture, as they understand it, on the Russian
peasants, seem equally to take as their rural
objective the replacement of small-scale by
large-scale cultivation.   This is perhaps easy
to understand in a country so primitively
under-farmed as many parts of Russia are
to-day; but it seems to me nevertheless a quite
wrong and unnecessary assumption. Socialism
is fully as compatible with small-scale cultivation as with large-scale " industrialised "
farming.

We should, then, both leave open the question of the scale on which farming will be conducted under Socialism, and make provision
in our schemes for the continuance of both
large and small farming under conditions in
accordance with our democratic principles.
We have thus a double problem to deal with
—the form of large-scale agriculture under
Guild Socialism, and the forms, and relation
to the large-scale system, of continuing
peasant cultivation.

Clearly, no considerable difficulty arises in
connection with the former type.   A National

Guild, decentralised and regionalised to a great extent, can undertake the control of large-scale agriculture quite as easily and naturally as of large-scale industry. There are likely, indeed, even on this side, to be certain differences between the functions and structure of an Agricultural Guild and those of the normal industrial Guild. For example, the members of the Guild who work on large farms and apply to their cultivation the latest scientific methods of large-scale production will almost certainly often have and work small individual holdings of their own in addition, and will draw from the Guild implements, manures and other requisites and assistance in the working of these holdings. Again, in a village almost wholly concerned in agricultural production, the Agricultural Guild might easily in many cases develop the functions not only of a producers' organisation and of a supply agency for agricultural requisites, but also of a general consumers' Co-operative Society, and might even admit into membership isolated villagers engaged, not directly in agriculture, but in some small-scale occupation ministering to rural needs. The village is, in many cases, so small a unit as not to require the same elaborate differentiation of functional bodies as larger aggregations of population require, and the Agricultural Guild, administered by forms of the most direct democracy, would naturally share with the Village Council a tendency to absorb the minor functions carried on within its area. Similar tendencies might be displayed, in a purely mining village, by the Miners' Guild.

With these important differences, however, the Agricultural Guild, so far as large-scale agriculture is concerned, would present almost exactly similar features to those common to other economic and service Guilds, possessing similar local, regional and national machinery, and similar forms of internal democratic control and self-management. The large-scale farm is as natural a unit of self-government as the factory, and a democracy extending to the local, regional and national organisation could as easily be based upon it.

Small-scale production presents a more difficult, largely because a less familiar, problem. It is at present carried on either by small holders or proprietors employing no one except members of their own family, or by small farmers, usually farming a rather larger area, and employing, though to a limited extent, hired labour. Can we contemplate at all, and, if so, under what conditions, the continuance of either or both of these forms of cultivation in a Guild Socialist Society? I at any rate, under the necessary safeguards, am fully prepared for the continuance of both to a considerable extent, not under their present conditions of isolation and purely individualised production, but with a full development of Co-operative methods and in integral connection with the Agricultural Guild.

There is manifestly no reason why a man should not, and every reason why he should, be free in a democratic Society to till a plot of land in his own way, subject to minimum safeguards as to proper use of the land. There is every reason why he should not be free to exploit the labour of his wife and children; but these are matters to be dealt with by social regulation by the whole community in the case of children, and in that of women, by women enjoying the economic and social independence which Guild Socialism must assure them. In a democratic Society, the object is the greatest freedom to every man to behave and produce as he chooses, consistently with social well-being; and there is every reason for believing that, especially where every acre counts and intensive production is important, the individual agricultural producer will have a large sphere of social usefulness, if not in the main forms of rural production, at any rate in many of its minor forms—market gardening, poultry farming, and the like.

The suggestion, however, that the individual holder should be tolerated on a scale which would entail the employment by him of "hired labour," or at any rate the labour on the farm of a number of individuals not being members of a single family, will, unless it is clearly understood, be likely to provoke considerable Socialist opposition. It is obviously desirable that, as far as possible, this form of production, where it persists, should be carried out not by one man employing others, but by an associated group of producers working together democratically with differences of function and recognised authority but not of social status. The small or middle-sized farm conducted on this principle could, in many cases, be directly a part of the Guild, and the associated producers on it could be a unit in the Guild organisation. But, just as we have provided for workshops remaining outside the Guilds, or only loosely connected with them, many farms conducted on the associative principle might occupy a similar position, bound to comply in certain respects with Guild regulations, and probably using the Guild, partly at least, as an agency for purchase and sale, but otherwise on their own. The Guild would thus tend to assume, for such farms, the functions of an Agricultural Co-operative Society, or, in some cases, these groups of associated producers might organise in Agricultural Co-operative Societies of their own, either federated with the Guild or separate from it.

This, however, still leaves to be faced the question of " hired labour." I simply do not feel that it is practicable to deny to the small-scale producers, whether individual or associative groups, all right to employ others. I feel,

however, that this right must be very strictly
safeguarded, and that the best safeguard—and
one that would arise naturally out of the
development of agricultural Trade Unionism
—is that all such labour should be supplied
only through and by the Guild, and under conditions as to the employment and status of the
workers concerned which the Guild itself
would lay down.   Probably such labour would
be almost entirely part-time labour required at
special seasons, and it might be largely that,
not of regular agricultural labourers, but either
of industrial workers harvesting or doing a
spell of rural work, or of small-holders giving
occasional help on the larger farms.   Such
workers, except where the relation was one of
friendship with an individual farmer, should
get their rural job through the Agricultural
Guild.

I envisage, then, a rural system including
both large- and small-scale forms of cultivation, conducted partly under the direct aus-
pices of an Agricultural Guild, largely decentralised and regionally administered, and
partly by individual producers or by associated
groups working more or less closely in conjunction with the Guild and under general Guild
regulations.   The closer this connection could
be made, and the more the Guild could combine with its direct organisation of production
the functions of an agricultural producers' Co-
operative Society in relation to small-scale

farmers, clearly the better for the smooth working of the dual system; and I believe the tendency under democratic conditions would be for the two methods, starting perhaps widely apart, to grow rapidly together. The Agricultural Guild would clearly be based mainly on the rural workers' Trade Unions of to-day, as the industrial and service Guilds will be based on Trade Union and professional organisations. The growth of an organisation capable of binding together the independent producers into a body capable of working in democratic association with the Agricultural Guild depends partly on the development of a democratic Agricultural Co-operative Movement not controlled, as the present British movement so largely is, by landowners and politicians, but expressing directly the point of view of the agricultural producers themselves. The Irish Agricultural Organisation Society is to a great extent such a movement already. The existence of such bodies is not at all inconsistent with the membership of most small-holders in the Agricultural Guild.

It is plain enough that the principal question of immediate practical importance which emerges from this outline of a possible democratic agricultural organisation is that of the position of the farmer. At present, where an organised agricultural proletariat exists, a serious struggle is beginning between it and the employing farmers, and the struggle shows every sign of reproducing in the countryside most of the features of the contest of capitalists and workers in industry. That to some extent this conflict is inevitable the determined opposition of most farmers to all attempts of the rural workers to establish reasonable conditions of life sufficiently shows; but it is nevertheless a mistake to equate the farmers as a class with the capitalists who dominate almost all important industries. The average farmer may be, and is, no better in mentality and outlook than the average industrial employer; but he is, on the average, a great deal his better in the fact that he is performing a useful social function more or less in the way in which it ought to be performed, and would continue to be performed in a democratic community. He exploits labour, it is true; but so does a Trade Union or a Co-operative Society. The point is that, under changed conditions and especially during the period of transition, the farmer will remain and perform a useful social service, when the industrial capitalist has disappeared.[2]

It is, in fact, a mistake to regard the farmers as a whole as a single and homogeneous social or economic class. This fact, under their very different conditions of widespread peasant cultivation, has been very definitely recognised

[2] The small industrial employer may, of course, also remain to some extent during the transition. Much the same considerations apply to him as to the farmer; but he bulks much less largely in industry than the farmer in agriculture.

by the Russian Communists, who have directed a great deal of energy to the detaching of the poorer cultivators from their former social subservience to the richer peasants.[3] Our problem is not the same; but other countries too have the task of bringing about a reflexion, in social organisation and economic allegiance, of the difference between the capitalist farmer who requires to be expropriated and the socially useful individual cultivator, who lives by his work and has no chance or prospect of accumulating riches or turning into a " country gentleman."   I believe the way to this recognition and change in outlook lies through the full recognition of the place of small- and middle-scale agriculture in the coming Society, and in the fostering of democratic organisation on producers' Co-operative lines among the smaller farmers as well as of Trade Unionism among the agricultural labourers.   The fissure can, of course, really come only in the ranks of the farmers themselves; but the possibility of its coming depends on the development by Socialists of a democratic agricultural policy in which the small farmer will see an assured place for himself.   I believe that Guild Socialism is broad and adaptable enough to provide this assurance; but I fully recognise that the problem requires far more detailed and expert working

[3] See the latter part of Lenin's book, *The Proletarian Revolution*, for the clearest exposition of Bolshevik land policy.

out than I have been able to attempt in this
chapter.   The actual and manifest tendency in
certain countries already, as in Canada and to
a less extent in the United States, in the
direction of an alliance between a large section
of organised farmers and the Trade Union
Movement encourages me to hope that, in
other countries also, a similar development is
not out of the question, however unpromising
at the moment, on a cursory survey of the
situation, its chances may appear to be.

CHAPTER X

EVOLUTION AND REVOLUTION

We have now completed our outline sketch of the structure and methods of working of a Guild Socialist Commonwealth, and have thus come to the threshold of the practical problem of transition to it from the capitalist Society of to-day. And here the first question that confronts us, as it confronts all Socialists under the conditions of the present time, is the question of " evolution and revolution." Do we hope and intend to bring about the great social transformation to which we look forward by purely evolutionary means, or do we anticipate, at some stage, a phase of catastrophic or revolutionary transition?

The question, stated, as it usually is, in that form, is to some extent misleading; for the word " revolutionary," and to a less extent the word " evolutionary " also, are capable of bearing a variety of interpretations. Revolution, or catastrophic transition, for example, though it probably always involves some employment of force, cannot be taken as necessarily involving force on a scale at all deserving the name of civil war. The first Russian Revolution of 1917 and the German Revolution of 1918 were both definitely revolutions, and were accompanied by some appeal to force; but in neither was force, in the sense of armed conflict, employed on any considerable scale. The old constitutional system which was displaced crumbled, and a different system took its place, with the minimum of fighting. There are, of course, many who contend that this is one of the main reasons why both these Revolutions achieved so little, and that real social revolution, involving a change of social and economic system as well as of political institutions, will never be accomplished save by a much more extensive employment of armed power; but, whether this is true or not, it is clearly necessary to distinguish between catastrophic change in which armed power, insofar as it exists, is only a secondary factor, and catastrophic change in which armed power is actually the principal agent of transformation.

Similarly, the word " evolutionary " has more than one sense. It is often interpreted to mean practically " political," and evolutionary methods are treated as identical with the constitutional employment of parliamentary action. But there is also a wider sense in which " evolutionary " tactics can denote a method applicable not merely to politics, but to every sphere of social action, economic and civic as well as political.

We shall do well, then, to re-state our question in a different form, or rather series of forms. First, we must ask whether constitutional political action alone affords a possible agent of social transformation, or whether it is even possible for the political changes involved in social transformation to retain throughout a consistently constitutional character. Secondly, we must ask whether evolutionary methods more widely conceived as including industrial and civic forms of Direct Action short of revolution can suffice to meet the needs of social transformation. If we are still unsatisfied, we must next enquire how far catastrophic action without civil war may be relied upon to meet the need, and, lastly, if need be, we must examine the chances and uses of civil war.

Throughout our examination of these issues, we must remember that it will be, to a great extent, not the challengers but the defenders of the capitalist system who will have the choice of weapons. Whatever methods Socialists, including Guild Socialists, may regard as the most hopeful for the attainment of the social reorganisation which they desire, it will always be possible for the defenders of capitalism, if they feel their position threatened, to appeal, successfully or unsuccessfully, to capitalist Direct Action or to armed force. And, usually though not universally, those against whom the extremer methods are employed have either to submit, or to retaliate by employing the same methods themselves. It is an obvious fact that capitalism will not stay quiet and do nothing while we mobilise our resources against it : in one way or another, it will struggle hard for its existence, and the tactics of its opponents will inevitably be guided, if not determined, by the tactics of its defenders.

Nor is it possible to anticipate that the question of methods will be decided by either party on a strictly rational basis. On both sides there is the factor of mob-psychology to be reckoned with ; and we have already seen enough to make us feel that, as we cannot rule out the possibility of an instinctive and irrational popular outbreak, so we can by no means be sure that the governing classes will not lose their heads and appeal to force out of sheer panic. For " Dyerism " at home and abroad is, like war itself, largely " the offspring of fear."

We cannot, then, sit in our chairs and lay down with scientific precision the strategy and tactics of the Guild Socialist, or of any great social, transformation. All we can do is to see what is the utmost, under the actual conditions, that any given method of action seems capable of achieving, and to make up our

minds not to use an extreme method if a less
extreme method promises to fulfil the same
purpose.   We can avoid revolution for revolution's sake ; but we cannot, even if we believe
that transformation without revolution is
practically possible, say that it will be so
accomplished.   For there are not merely two
parties to the struggle, each with a will of its
own—there is also a very powerful third party,
which we may call, according to our taste,
either chance or fate.

It is, however, worth while, with all these
considerations in mind, and with the accomplished fact of the Russian Revolution before
us, to consider what is the utmost possible
capacity of the various methods that are proposed for our adoption in changing the face of
Society.   Let us enquire first, then, what is
the utmost that we can hope to get by the use
of constitutional political action.   It is of no
advantage, in this connection, to count up the
total number of more or less working-class
voters, and to point out that it is theoretically
possible for these voters to return a working-
class Government that means business, and for
the Government, under our elastic constitutional arrangements, to transform the whole
organisation of Society.   It is of no advantage
because, in the first place, there is no chance
under capitalism of the whole working-class
voting together, or of a really " class-conscious " majority returning to power a really

"class-conscious" Government; because, in the second place, this Government, if it could exist, would find the change impossible to achieve in less than a century by parliamentary methods; because, in the third place, the existing State organisation is quite unsuited to the execution of any purpose involving fundamental structural changes in Society; and because, in the fourth place, the attempt to bring about the transformation by political means alone would almost inevitably, long before its completion, provoke a counter-revolutionary movement by the governing classes, based on their power in the economic sphere. The period required to convert, in opposition to the whole force of money-directed education, propaganda and pressure, a majority of the people to a habit of sound political thinking is a sufficient reason against the practicability of social transformation by this means; for long before the culmination of the process the present economic system would have fallen in ruins owing to the operation of other causes already defined in this book. I do not mean that it might not be possible, and even easy, before long to secure a Labour Government; but I mean that such a Government would probably arrive at power only if it were certain in advance that it would not even attempt any radical social transformation, and would in any case find the task of accomplishing such a transformation almost insuperably difficult.

Indeed, a Labour Government would be far more likely to come as a brake than as a spur.

The fundamental reason why political methods alone will not do for the purpose of radical social transformation is that the transformation required is fundamentally not political but economic. It is undeniably true that, under the capitalist system, "economic power precedes political power." It is the object of Guild Socialists to destroy this predominance of economic factors; but that only makes them the more conscious of its existence to-day. It is the economic, rather than the political, power of the workers that will avail to overthrow capitalism; and, while this economic power may at times assume a political expression, it will operate mainly within its own sphere. The utmost, then, that we can expect of working-class political action is that it should serve to support the exercise of working-class economic power, and to ease and smooth a transition which it is impotent actually to accomplish. Properly understood, this may be an important secondary function; but it is no more.

We have, then, to consider carefully the other methods of evolutionary action which are at the disposal of the working-class movement. With some of these we shall be dealing more fully in the next chapter; but we can here discuss them in general terms. Clearly, the most important is the direct manifestation of working-class economic power, based on the control which the working-class organisations possess over the labour-power of their members. This may take the form on occasion of " direct action " for a political purpose ; but its normal exercise is for definitely economic ends. It is the instrument by the use of which the Trade Union Movement has not only increased wages and improved conditions, but also greatly raised the status of the workers and established already a considerable measure of negative and external control over industry. Clearly this process can be pushed considerably further, as it is indeed being pushed further by one Union or another every day. The Unions can extend, and are extending, the amount of their control over industry, and in some cases, as in the miners' scheme of public ownership and democratic control or the direct constructive experiments of the Building Guilds, are already putting forward claims whose realisation would result in an important transformation of the productive control of industry.

There is, however, clearly a limit to this process. It can be used to wrest the control of the productive operations of industry largely from the hands of the capitalists, and even, in some cases, to bring about the substitution of public for private ownership. It can, in the form of " Direct Action " as it is now understood, be used for the furtherance of isolated demands of an even more far-reaching character, extending to considerable inroads on the rights of property. But I do not see how, either alone or in combination with the political weapon or with other evolutionary weapons, such as the conquest of power in local government and the maximum development of working-class education, it can be made an instrument of complete social transformation, or of the central process in that transformation —the actual wresting from the rich of their wealth and economic power.

In other words, a revolutionary element is unavoidable in any " thorough " policy of social transformation.   But it is none the less clear that the maximum development of the evolutionary policy, especially on its economic and industrial side, would not merely make the chances of the success of any " revolutionary " action infinitely greater, but would tend to reduce to the minimum the amount of " revolutionary " action required.   Before developing this point, let us look for a moment at the possibilities of " revolutionary " action taken by itself, or rather based upon the present strength and organisation of the working-class movement.

If we assume the " class-conscious " elements among the workers to have made up their minds, as some among them have, that immediate " revolutionary " action is required, what line of policy would it be natural for them to pursue? They would presumably not attempt to provoke an outbreak in reliance purely on the deliberate revolutionaries among the workers, but would pursue the process of educating, organising and extending the revolutionary minority, and would lie in wait to seize their chance to base a revolutionary movement on some widespread industrial or "direct action" crisis. They would, in the meantime, naturally use every effort to improve the organisation of Labour and to persuade it to assume more militant tactics. So far they would agree; but at this point a difference might arise among them as to the meaning of the word "revolution." Some would conceive of it as a sort of extension of "direct action"—a paralysing of the economic life of Society through the general strike, resulting in the dislocation and collapse of its political machinery. Others would conceive of it as actually assuming the form of civil war. Let us take the latter possibility first.

Real civil war can only be conducted when both parties to the conflict are armed. The arming of the workers, however, could not possibly be accomplished in either Great Britain or America, whatever may be the case in Germany or Italy, until and unless the process of dissolution and decay of the capitalist system and of its political machinery has proceeded much further than it has at present. A revolt of the Army, which seems the only alternative, is most improbable as the result of any revolutionary propaganda, and would only be at all likely to occur if, when a revolutionary situation had arisen from apparently non-revolutionary causes, soldiers were asked to shoot persons whom they regarded as harmless fellow-citizens. It might occur in such circumstances; but this would come about not through the efforts of the revolutionaries, but for reasons which they are almost powerless to influence. This is very widely recognised, and few who call themselves revolutionaries have much faith in the results of deliberately provoking a civil war for which they have no means of preparing.

The second alternative, envisaged by those who regard revolution as extended " Direct Action," is more plausible, but leaves, at present, far too much to providence. It depends for its success on the power of the workers, by means of their industrial organisation, without first starving themselves out, to hold up the economic mechanism of Society for a long enough time to cause the political and economic structure of the present system to fall in ruins. This, I believe, would be possible for a Labour Movement possessing the present strength of our own, only in face of a capitalist Society far less strong than our own, and only at a quite exceptionally favourable moment, such as occurred in Russia in 1917. To overthrow by this means the far stronger capitalism of Great Britain or America would require a very much stronger, and more fully awakened, Labour Movement than now exists in either country.

The working-class that would do this would have to be, not only stronger in itself—that is, in numbers, organisation, determination, and clear vision of policy—but also more strongly entrenched.   In other words, it would need to have carried the evolutionary processes with which we have dealt already much further than they have yet been carried; for the processes, while they are by themselves essentially inadequate for the task of radical social transformation, are the necessary precursors of any successful revolutionary action.   In the most successful *émeute* that can be conceived of to-day, the workers would be confronted with the immediate and imperative necessity of occupying simultaneously many thousand strategic points—not merely of seizing power at the centre and improvising a Provisional Government, but of seizing thousands of local civic bodies, of taking over and improvising administrations in many thousands of factories —of learning in a day a thousand lessons of self-mastery and communal service.   I do not say that it could not be done; but I say that its doing would be a miracle.

The further, however, the workers can carry, without sacrificing the ideal of radical transformation, the evolutionary process of detailed conquest of power in each sphere, and above all in the spheres of industry and local government, the less insuperable these objections appear.   Development of Trade Union membership, organisation and education extends and improves the fighting force : development of Co-operation improves the rationing facilities[1] : conquest of power in local government simplifies the administrative transition, and places important economic services in the workers' hands : the extension of Trade Union control weakens the capitalists' hold on the factories, and helps to teach the workers how to run industry themselves.   He who wishes revolution to succeed should hasten towards it slowly, and prepare the way for it by detailed conquests.

But, as I made clear at the outset, it is the challenged who chooses the weapons, and we cannot be sure that our ordered advance will proceed according to plan.   Least of all can any group of workers in Europe be sure of this in face of the steady disorganisation of the European economic and political system which was hastened rather than arrested by the Peace of Versailles.   At any moment, it is at least possible that a revolutionary situation may arise, either because the possessing classes think that the moment for resistance has come,

[1] Co-operative Societies, by assuring food supplies, have already given considerable help in trade disputes, as in the Dublin strike of 1913-4, and the Railway Strike of 1919.   This help is capable of being very greatly extended.

or because the contending parties have merely
muddled themselves into a situation from
which there is no other outlet. If such a movement were to come soon, I do not, unless the
circumstances were almost unbelievably
favourable, cherish much hope of a working-
class success on the first occasion ; but neithei
have I any fear of a lasting working-class
defeat. I believe, however, that the vast
majority of class-conscious workers will have
no desire to tempt these perils unless they are
convinced that no alternative is open to them.

Especially for Guild Socialists, who have not
only a positive ideal but a definite evolutionary
programme, it seems clear that the thing to
aim at—whether we can in fact attain to it or
not—is not early revolution, but the consolida-
tion of all forces on the lines of evolutionary
development with a view to making the " revolution," which in one sense must come, as
little as possible a civil war and as much as possible a registration of accomplished facts and a
culmination of tendencies already in operation.
The complete change which we desire could
not be carried through wholly by constitutional means, industrial or political, even if the
governing classes were to allow the developments which undermined their power to proceed to the end without resisting them by
force ; but at the best the unconstitutional
" revolution " might be reduced to a mere
clearing away of what had already become use-

less débris of a decayed system, and the rapid
organisation into a recognised social system
of forces and institutions which had already
attained under capitalism to considerable
powers and functions by methods of encroachment. If we cannot achieve this, and if revolution, owing to the resistance of the possessing classes, comes more quickly than we get
ready for it, and therefore assumes a more
forcible character, we shall be all the better prepared in proportion to the advances which we
have made by the method of encroachment up
to the time of its arrival.   The policy which I
am advocating must, if it is to succeed, be not
slow, but rapid : it is, however, gradual, in the
literal sense, that it proceeds by steps.   It will
not appeal to those who seek to model their
conduct blindly on the Russian Revolution ;
but I do not believe that, unless quite unfore-
seen circumstances arise, Russian methods can
be applied either to the British or to the
American situation.

CHAPTER XI

THE POLICY OF TRANSITION

THE two great working-class movements—
Trade Unionism and Co-operation—on which
I have dwelt so much in the foregoing chapters,
have both made remarkable progress during
the last few years. Nor is there any considerable doubt that this progress will continue;
for both movements fulfil purposes which a
growing proportion of the workers recognise
as essential. There are, however, in both cases
obvious checks on this advance. Trade
Unionism thrives on good trade rather than on
bad, and, even apart from this fact, its very
success is constantly bringing it face to face
with more formidable obstacles, and notably,
just at present, with a growing determination
of the possessing classes either to tame it into
acceptance of capitalism or to crush it if they
cannot. In the case of Co-operation, which
is as yet, despite its theorists, in practice a far

less ambitious movement, the main check is imposed by the fact that Co-operation, working under capitalist conditions, depends for its advance on securing adequate capital by voluntary means.   As members' share capital increases but slowly, a sudden accession of membership may easily mean that there is not enough capital available from this source to finance the necessary expansions, still less to do the pioneering work required to bring about a further widening of the movement.   The Co-operative Wholesale Society, confronted with this problem, recently resorted to the debatable expedient of raising debentures in the open market—a course which, though the interest was fixed, would obviously have a tendency to assimilate it further to capitalist concerns.   Even if this expedient is employed, there can be no doubt that the problem of capital is by itself quite enough to prevent the Co-operative Movement, however it may expand in the sphere of distribution, from seriously challenging within any measurable period the domination of capitalism over production.   Its productive achievements are startling enough when they are compared even with those of the largest individual capitalist firms; but they are very small indeed in comparison with the volume of competing capitalist enterprise as a whole.

There are ways of mitigating, but not of removing, this obstacle to the expansion of the

Co-operative Movement under capitalism. The fuller utilisation of working-class resources for Co-operative development would do something, but not enough; for Co-operators are faced by the fact that it is simply not possible, at least within any measurable period, to drive the possessing classes out of industry simply by competing with them under conditions which these classes themselves prescribe.   Moreover, Co-operation, if it were really dangerous to large-scale capitalism, would probably soon learn that the possessing classes have still the power, if they think it necessary, to alter the competitive conditions to suit themselves.   The attempts to tax Co-operative Societies may be regarded as a slight foretaste of such a policy.

It is, however, clear that, as long as Co-operation continues along its present lines, the main assault upon the strongholds of capitalism will not be its handiwork.   It may, and certainly will, help by placing its resources more fully at the disposal of its members who are engaged in the combat and of the Trade Union Movement as a whole; but it is upon the Trade Unions that the brunt of the struggle will fall.   It is upon our success in laying the foundations of the Guild even under capitalism that the chances of Guild Socialism really depend, and the problem of the transition to Guild Socialism is therefore primarily a problem of Trade Union development.

It is not possible here to describe in detail the stage of development and of positive achievement which Trade Unionism has now reached. It has expanded its membership to the point of being practically blackleg-proof among the manual workers in many of the leading industries, and especially in those which are of the greatest strategic importance. There are six and a half, and probably more nearly seven, million Trade Unionists, and these include nearly all the most important elements amongst the manual workers, with an increasing, though still relatively small, proportion of non-manual workers as well. New classes of workers are rapidly organising, especially among the latter, and gradually the " black-coated " are realising the expediency of throwing in their lot with the manual workers in their struggle. Moreover, the Trade Unions have achieved a large amount of negative control over industry through the method of collective bargaining, and, strategically most important of all, are rapidly reaching the point at which they can, if they will, make the capitalist system, if not unworkable, at all events very uncomfortable to work and to live under.

There are, however, considerable weaknesses still apparent in Trade Unionism, formidable as it has become. There is still no coherent plan of Trade Union organisation, and no considered policy accepted either by the movement as a whole, or by the dominant sections within it.   Unions quarrel fiercely one with another about all manner of questions, but above all about membership and demarcation; and, when it is with the employers that they quarrel, the lack of constructive proposals and demands is often the most notable feature of their programme.   They literally do not know what to ask for, or at least have, for the most part, not yet learned to translate vague aspirations into actual and definite proposals capable of immediate enforcement.

There are, then, at least four respects in which the Trade Union Movement requires fundamental reorganisation in order to fit itself for any considerable further advance—most of all if that advance is to be directed to making the Trade Unions of to-day the basis of the Guilds of to-morrow.   In the first place, the basis of membership must be effectively broadened, not only by the inclusion of the non-manual workers, but by a definite and formal recognition of their distinctive position in the conduct of industry.   Secondly, the basis of organisation must be settled, and the Trade Union Movement changed from a congeries of mutually suspicious and often conflicting units into a rationally organised body, following in the main the " industrial " form of organisation, and binding together the whole of the Trade Unionist workers into a single effectively directed force, really capable

of united action on matters of common concern.   Thirdly, the internal government of
the Unions needs to be democratised by the
recognition of the workshop, or its equivalent,
as the essential basis of organisation, on which
the larger units of administration ought to be
built up.   And fourthly, the Trade Union
Movement needs a clear and definite policy,
the same in its fundamental principles for all
workers, but admitting of wide variations
according to the nature and circumstances of
each industry and group.   Moreover, such a
policy must have two aspects.   It must indicate the right demands to make upon
employers in industrial negotiations, and it
must also give clear guidance as to the attitude
of the workers towards the State, not only as
employers, but in all the various aspects in
which it faces Labour.

These four aspects of Trade Union reorganisation hang very closely together, and
their realisation is to a great extent interdependent.   But it is mainly the last—the
question of policy—upon which the others
depend; for the only power strong enough to
enable the obstacles to internal Trade Union
reorganisation and the firm union of workers
by hand and brain to be overcome is the presence of a clearly-realised objective, requiring
for its attainment a policy based upon these
changes of structure, administration, and attitude.   It is, for example, comparatively easy

to create the mechanism of a Trade Union
" General Staff " ; but it is far less easy to
make it work unless there is a clear conception
of the object for which it is working. It is
easy to plan ideal schemes either for " One
Big Union," or for " union by industry " ;
but the impulse required to carry such schemes
into effect will come only with the realisation
that craft Unionism is incapable of achieving
real control in industry, and that not only can
" Industrial Unions " or the sections of " One
Big Union " quarrel among themselves, but
the mere form of organisation is nothing without the spirit and the purpose behind it.

It would take a whole book, and not merely
a single comparatively brief chapter, to give
any full indication of the nature of the changes
required in Trade Union organisation under
the first three heads which I have mentioned,
and I shall not here attempt any such impossible task. To a great extent the problem
has to be faced for itself by each industry ; but
even an exposition of the general principles
involved would take us too far afield.[1] I must
therefore content myself with pointing out
that, if Trade Unions are to serve as the basis
of Guilds, (1) they must clearly be organised on
industrial lines, so as to include all the necessary workers in each industry, whether by hand

---

[1] I have written a good deal about this problem elsewhere. See
especially my *Self-Government in Industry*, chapter III. R. Page Arnot's
pamphlet, *Trade Unionism: a New Model* (I.L.P., 2d.), contains a very
useful brief treatment of the problem.

or by brain, and so as, in addition, to recognise, within each Union, the distinctions of function among the different grades and sections of workers, and (2), if in the Guilds a democracy based upon the natural unit of the workers' industrial consciousness—the factory or workshop, or its equivalent—is required, this kind of democracy is not a whit less necessary in the Trade Unions of to-day.

I wish, however, to devote the remainder of this chapter, not to a consideration of the internal problems of Trade Unionism, but to the policy which Trade Unions need to adopt if they desire to take the first steps towards the establishment of the Guild Socialist Society described in this book.   In the last chapter, this policy, so far as it relates to working-class action " under capitalism " or " before the revolution," as it is variously described, was briefly characterised as a policy of encroachment.[2]

By " encroaching control " is meant a policy directed to wresting bit by bit from the hands of the possessing classes the economic power which they now exercise, by a steady transference of functions and rights from their nominees to representatives of the working-class.   It is not the same as " joint control," with which it is sometimes confused ; for

---

[2] I have endeavoured to work out in detail the essentials of this policy, as applied to most of the principal industries, in my book, *Chaos and Order in Industry*. I am here only restating in very general terms my main conclusions.

" joint control " aims at the co-operative
exercise of certain functions by employers and
employed, whereas " encroaching control "
aims at taking certain powers right out of the
employers' hands, and transferring them completely to the organised workers. A quite
simple instance will plainly illustrate this
fundamental difference. " Joint control "
involves joint works committees, on which
employer and employed work together:
" encroaching control " involves Trade Union
shop stewards' committees, which the
employer has to recognise, but to which
neither he nor any representative of his
interests is admitted. The latter, of course,
need not be quarrelling all the time with the
employer; but they must remain strictly independent of him. There is, indeed, between
" Whitleyism " or " joint control " and
Guild Socialist policy, or " encroaching
control," all the difference between depend-
ence and independence. It is, moreover, vital
that the shop stewards' committees should be
integral parts of the Trade Unions, and should
regard themselves as the representatives, in
their particular factories, of the wider working-class movement outside.

The right course, then, for the Trade
Unions, at least in dealing with the private
employer, is to endeavour, as far as possible,
to wrest and take over from him any function
which they feel strong enough to assume and

to exercise unaided.   Such functions may be
great or small; but every such exclusive
assumption of power represents a real gain,
and brings the workers a real step nearer to
industrial self-government, which involves the
complete assumption of the capitalists' power
by the representatives of producers and consumers.   Of course, this gain would not be
made if any function were assumed on conditions—such as those of profit-sharing—which
would entangle the workers in the capitalist
system.   It must therefore be further laid
down that the control assumed must be not
only in itself exclusive control, but such as to
help the workers towards the assumption of
further powers, without in any way entangling
them in the capitalist order.

This guiding principle of industrial policy
requires, of course, to be worked out in as
many different ways as there are industries and
sets of economic circumstances.   Here I can
only mention a few of the more obvious appli-
cations.   First, just as Trade Unionism requires reorganisation on a workshop basis, the
workshop obviously provides the most natural
first point of the Trade Union attack; for it
is in the workshop that the workers can most
easily concentrate their power and take over
positive functions, and it is there that the most
important outposts, though by no means the
citadels of capitalism lie.   In the workshop
therefore the organised workers, acting in

accordance with plans laid by their Unions, should aim at seizing all the power they can, chiefly by two closely related means—first, by taking from the employer and transferring to themselves the right to appoint workshop supervisors, foremen and the like, and so making the discipline of the shop a matter, no longer of imposition from without, but of self-regulation by the group as a whole; and, secondly, by substituting as far as possible for the present individual relationship of the employer to each worker, whom he, through his representatives, hires, fires, and re-munerates individually, a collective relation to the employer of all the workers in the shop, so that the necessary labour is in future sup-plied by the Union, and the workers substitute their own collective regulations for " hiring and firing " for those of the employer, and, wherever possible, enter into a collective con-tract with him to cover the whole output of the shop, and themselves, according to their own Union regulations, apportion the work and share out the payment received.

This policy as a whole has come to be known by the name of *Collective Contract*.   Guilds-men do not pretend that it is equally applicable to all industries and conditions, and they admit that it has been based mainly on the conditions which exist in the engineering and kindred in-dustries.   They hold, however, that it is in large measure capable of application to all

" factory " industries, and that almost every type of worker can apply one or more of its proposals to his own case. There is at any rate no type of workers who cannot claim the right to elect their own supervisors, to assume some sort of control of " hiring and firing," and, in a number of respects, to substitute a collective relation of all the workers employed, acting as a Trade Union group, for the individual relation of each worker to the firm.

Again, an obvious line of advance in all industries is for the Trade Unions directly to insist that, as the unemployed constitute the " reserve of labour " of the various industries and services, the principle of " industrial maintenance " administered by the Trade Unions shall be established to cover cases both of complete unemployment and of underemployment in the forms of " standing off " and " short time." In other words, the maintenance of the unemployed at their customary standard of life should be recognised as a legitimate charge upon the various industries ; and the insecurity of discontinuous employment, which is one of the " stigmata " of wage-slavery, should thus be removed from the workers. The agitation for this change has already made considerable headway in the Trade Union world, and the establishment of the principle of " industrial maintenance " would be obviously a step towards the abolition of the wage-system and the establishment of Guild Socialism.[3]

The workers in the building industry, thanks to the special position and nature of the industry itself, have recently been able to advance considerably further than workers in most other services are for the present able to go. The building industry, because of the acute housing shortage, occupies a position especially favourable to new experiments, and is, in addition, of such a nature that the element of " fixed capital " is, in relation to the greater part of its work, of far less importance than in other large-scale industries. If the working capital for pay, materials and a comparatively modest amount of plant can be secured, large operations in the building of working-class houses can be carried through almost without fixed capital. Taking advantage of this opportunity, the building operatives of Manchester, guided by Mr. S. G. Hobson, and speedily followed by those of other centres, were able to take the step of actually founding Building Guilds and Guild Committees, which, with their command of the necessary labour power, could undertake to build houses directly for the local authorities, thus eliminating altogether the building trade employer and his search for profits, and

[3] See for this question of Unemployment, S. G. Hobson's *Guild Principles in War and Peace*, my *Self-Government in Industry* (chapter IV) and Reckitt and Bechhofer's *The Meaning of National Guilds* (chapter IX)

at the same time ensuring to the Guild members full maintenance by the Guild as long as they continued of its fellowship. It is too early yet to judge whether this experiment will achieve the great practical success which it deserves; for it has to contend with the acute hostility not only of the master builders, but also of most local authorities and of the bureaucracy, which are, of course, still mainly dominated by the capitalist point of view. There is, indeed, good reason to hope that it will surmount even these obstacles, and thus furnish, while the capitalist system remains in existence, a working model of a large part of a great industry conducted without profit and under conditions of industrial self-government. Whatever befalls it, the force of the example will not be lost, and other workers will be able to learn from this courageous pioneering experiment in industrial democracy.

Of course, no one contends that, even if the Building Guilds meet with success, they can, as long as they are ringed round by a hostile capitalist environment in both industry and politics, really be " Guilds " of the kind which Guild Socialists desire to establish. They can be at best only pale foreshadowings of the Guilds, and they will inevitably be driven to some compromises in their hard struggle with capitalism. But the essential principles for which they stand are clear. They refuse to treat the labour of a human being as a commodity that can be bought and sold on ordinary commercial principles, and they therefore insist on full maintenance of all their members, in sickness and in health, in work or out of work. They refuse to make a profit; and therefore insist on building at cost, including the maintenance of their members as a legitimate factor in cost. They refuse to admit the principle of control from outside and above, and base themselves on the principle of self-government, the free association for service of all grades of workers by hand or brain who are necessary fc.' the work in hand. These are essential features of the Guild, and the Building Guilds are the first attempt, in face of very real difficulties, to give them a concrete shape.

But, it may be asked, if there is this simple and peaceable way of creating Guilds, without any direct expropriation of anybody or any violent upheaval, why cannot the workers in other industries follow the example of the builders, and so avoid all need for social revolution or class warfare? There are two simple but definite reasons why they cannot. In the first place, there is hardly another industry that is like the building industry in requiring practically no fixed capital for a great deal of its work. Most industries are carried on in costly factories, in mines upon the development of which large sums have been spent, in privately-owned work-places which would have to be transferred to the workers' possession before they could begin to produce except for the owners' profit. Builders indeed often have workshops, and big structural jobs require fixed capital; but ordinary house-building can be carried on with practically no fixed capital if the client is in a position to pay over the purchase-price as the work proceeds and as the bills for plant and materials have to be met. This is how the ordinary builder builds; but it is not how the ordinary mineowner or engineering[4] firm produces. Secondly, the building operatives are able to make their offer with some hope of its being accepted mainly because both private and State "enterprise" are so manifestly failing to produce the houses which the people need, despite heavy financial inducements and one Housing Act after another. It should therefore be difficult for local authorities in whose areas the need is great and the provision scanty, to reject under present conditions the offers of the Building Guilds, at least where there is any organised public opinion in the area to keep them "straight."

Other industries offer to the workers a very different prospect. The miners, for example, when they desire to take a real step towards the establishment of a Mining Guild, cannot leave their employers and begin mining on

---

4 Engineering, of course, stands on a different footing from mining as well as from building. For a discussion of the engineering problem, see my *Chaos and Order in Industry*, chapter VIII.

their own, because all the mines are privately owned. They have to demand public ownership, not because they want the State to manage the mines, but as the only way of getting rid of the mineowners and at least clearing the path for the creation of a Mining Guild. They know that State management would be inefficient and bad both for the consumer and for the miner; and they therefore couple with their demand for public ownership a demand for democratic control. They cannot, however, even under public ownership, hope, in face of bureaucratic and capitalist opposition, to proceed at once to a Mining Guild; and they have therefore to put forward a proposal for joint control with the State, which would at least be a step towards it. This is possible, whereas joint control with the mineowner is not, because under public ownership, however capitalistic the State may be, direct private profiteering in the industry is at least eliminated.

The position of the miners is almost identical with that of other workers who are demanding the " nationalisation " of their industries. They do this, not because they want or believe in State management of industry, but in order, by clearing the private owner out of the way, to open the road to Guild or workers' control.

It is true, of course, that nationalisation, carried out under capitalism, does not really

abolish private ownership, but only changes
the private property claim from a varying
claim on the profits of a particular industry to
a fixed claim on the national resources as a
whole. This, however, is of advantage, both
because it makes the adoption of a reasonable
form of control possible in the nationalised
industry, and also because, by reducing the
capitalist to a mere obviously functionless
bondholder or *rentier*, it makes far easier the
subsequent annihilation of his claim, which
ceases to have even the apparent relation to
social service arrogated to it at present. If
the workers could secure in the vital industries
what the miners demand, that is, public
ownership with at least a half share in control for themselves, they would have at the
same time greatly strengthened their position for further onslaughts upon the capitalist
system, and have weakened capitalism by
depriving it, not indeed of its wealth, but of
the economic functions and powers upon
which the retention of that wealth in the long
run depends.

In short, the real aim of the organised
workers, and the keynote of Trade Union
policy, must be not merely the expropriation
of the capitalist, but the supersession of his
economic functions and his replacement by
the workers in every sphere of his economic
and social power. For it is by this capture
and assumption of social and economic func-

tions that the workers will alone make possible an equitable distribution of the national income and a reasonable reorganisation of Society as a whole. The essential method of Guild Socialism is the replacement of the capitalist by the worker in every strategic position, whether it be in industry or commerce or in those governmental functions which it is necessary to capture in order either to re-create or to destroy.

CHAPTER XII

THE INTERNATIONAL OUTLOOK

AT the end of this exposition of the theory and policy of Guild Socialism, there is a question which obviously suggests itself. Both the theory and the policy which I have been describing have been developed in Great Britain and in direct relation to British conditions. Are they, or are they not, of more general application? In other words, is Guild Socialism put forward as a scheme claiming the same validity as, for example, Socialism itself claims, or as the Guild system possessed in the Middle Ages?

It is hard to answer either "Yes" or "No" to that question. There is already evidence enough that Guild Socialism is likely to have a widespread and largely similar appeal among all the English-speaking peoples—in the United States of America, in Australasia and in South Africa, hardly less than in the United Kingdom. There is also a close resemblance between it and movements which exist, at many different stages of development, in various countries on the Continent of Europe; but in these cases the variations are markedly greater, and the workers in these countries are more likely to come to similar conclusions as a result of quite distinct mental processes than directly to adopt the Guild Socialist idea. In the English-speaking countries, if Guild Socialism is adopted, it will almost certainly be with important divergences from the present theory, suggested in part by the difference in material conditions and in part by national differences of temperament and tradition.

This is as it should be. Guild Socialists, who do not want any two Guilds, or any two districts of one Guild, to be the same, certainly do not want all countries to be organised rigidly under a uniform system. They have taken into their plan as much as they could of British tradition and temperament, and they recognise fully that each country must work out its social salvation for itself and on its own lines. But they believe that the essential principles on which Guild Socialism rests, as they provide solutions for difficulties which are almost universal, have a message wherever these difficulties exist. These principles admit of the foundation upon them of many different forms of social structure, and, even for their own country, Guild Socialists are not foolish enough to flatter themselves that they have devised in all respects that which is best. The principles are there, to be

14

applied according to traditions and conditions in many diverse ways, or even themselves to be substantially modified.

If the world is to live at peace—and not merely at peace, but in a real international relation of fellowship and co-operation—it is essential that the various social systems existing within it, while retaining great national differences, should be homogeneous enough in the principles on which they rest to admit of really cordial common action. Between real democracies and real tyrannies there can be no true co-operation, whatever interchange of commodities and opinions there may be. It is essential to the security and best working of a Guild Socialist Society that it should exist in a world which, if it is not Guild Socialist, consists mainly of communities which possess, in one form or another, a social structure that makes for freedom. This is true more than ever to-day, when the relations between nations are necessarily so close that evil in one cannot but communicate itself in some measure to others. Guild Socialists look forward, then, to a world of free Societies, and visualise the complete establishment of Guild Socialism only in such an environment.

This makes it a matter for them of the first importance what tendencies are developing among the working-classes of other countries. Wherever they look, they are encouraged to find, not merely similar problems awaiting solution, but at the least largely similar instincts stirring among the workers and in many cases theories similar to their own in the air. Naturally, they have watched eagerly the internal Russian situation, as far as " sanitary cordons " and the constant garbling of news by capitalist agencies and journals allow them to do so. They realise, of course, that the present conduct of Russian industry is dominated almost wholly by the necessities of war, and that it would be absurd to look, in the present situation, for the development of any clearly devised democratic industrial system. They realise also that the Russian Communists, not unnaturally, value the security of their Revolution more than they value immediate attempts at stimulating democratic self-government among the imperfectly educated and recently emancipated workers of Russia. They understand the temptation, under present conditions, to fall back upon " iron working-class discipline " as easier than democracy ; but they realise that this, bad as it is, may be only a passing phase of the Revolution, made inevitable by the military adventures and the *cordon sanitaire* of the Allied Powers. Even so, they find that, despite the nominal " State Sovereignty " of the Soviets, economic powers and functions have in fact passed mainly into the hands of quite distinct economic bodies, co-ordinated by the Supreme Council of National Economy, which, like the lesser bodies, consists mainly of Trade Union representatives. They find that what Lenin means when he says that the Trade Unions have become "State organisations" is not that they have been subordinated and made mere instruments for the execution of Soviet decrees, but that they have entered into the recognised constitution of Society, and have assumed, to a great extent, their proper functional place in the direction of the productive processes of industry. Similarly, they find that the so-called "nationalisation" of the Co-operative Societies, so far from destroying their power or merging them in the Soviets, seems to be resulting in their reorganisation as the constitutionally recognised representatives of all the consumers, exercising functions closely resembling those which Guild Socialists would assign to the Co-operative Movement in the future.

It is, no doubt, true that Sovietism, or rather Bolshevism, under the stress of war, which has largely absorbed the younger men, shows at present a marked bureaucratic tendency by no means in harmony with Guild Socialist ideas; but the most competent observers agree in holding, and in stating that Lenin holds, that, when once the pressure of necessity is removed, the bureaucracy and the "State-like" Soviets will together atrophy so far as economic functions are concerned, leaving the Trade Unions and the consumers' organisations in possession of the economic field. Such a system would not be so far removed from Guild Socialism as to make the closest international relationships difficult.

Over Europe, at present, the cry is going up from the " left wing " in every country for " the Soviet system and the dictatorship of the proletariat." This cry is really neither more nor less than the cry for an early social revolution of the workers. But with it is mingled everywhere a cry, less clearly articulate perhaps but unmistakeable, of the producers for industrial freedom and self-government. This cry is heard in Germany largely intermingled with the Communist demand, and attempts to circumvent it play a large part in the German semi-capitalist " socialisation " schemes, which are the equivalent of " Whitleyism " as expressed in the mining and railway proposals of the British Government. Everywhere not only are the workers organising to secure power over the State : they are also putting forward a plain demand, however little it may be expressed in a formal theory, for self-government in the sphere of industry.

Two other cases at which we must glance are those of France and the United States of America. France was the original home of " Syndicalism," a blending of Anarchist Communism with Trade Unionism from which Guild Socialists learnt much in the early days

of their own movement. The Syndicalist
impulse spread far and wide before the war,
and, though it did not plant itself as an organised movement outside the Latin countries, was an important factor in the industrial
awakening of ten or so years ago. In France
itself, it seemed to have spent its force of
ideas just at the time when it was producing
its greatest effects abroad; but it has recently
been shown that its impulse is still fruitful and
that it is taking a new shape under the changed
conditions of the present time. The formula
for which the French workers by hand and
brain, united in the Economic Council of
Labour, are now contending is "industrialised
nationalisation," by which is meant public
ownership of industry together with a system
of joint control by the representatives of producers and consumers. This proposal is not
Guild Socialism; but it is closely enough allied
to it to make co-operation between two communities founded, the one upon Guild Socialist
ideas and the other on the new French Labour
policy, not merely easy, but certain and in-
frangible.

Still less is the "Plumb Plan,"[1] first prepared for the American Railroad Brother-
hoods, and subsequently endorsed by the
miners and by other groups of American
workers, to be identified with Guild Socialism;
but it also is founded on some at least of the

[1] For a full discussion of the "Plumb Plan" see my *Chaos and Order in Industry*, chapter VI.

same essential principles. It is a plan for the public ownership and democratic control of industry, differing from the British plans in important respects, and above all in its retention in a modified form of material incentives to efficient service. I myself believe this particular provision to be unfortunate and unnecessary; but I recognise all the same that the " Plumb Plan " is first cousin, if not brother, to some of the proposals advocated in this book.

These are only instances chosen from a very much larger number, to which additions are constantly being made in one country or another.[2] I believe that the impulses and reasonings which are at present moving to action the workers in almost all the industrial countries, are throughout sufficiently similar to be certain, if the workers succeed in overthrowing capitalism, of establishing social systems alike enough to work easily together. I am, moreover, fairly sure that nearly all these systems will in large measure embody most of the vital principles for which Guild Socialists stand, however much the actual methods of giving effect to these principles may differ from case to case. I am not, therefore, troubled by the nightmare of a Guild Socialist community ringed round by hostile nations, or much perturbed by the difficulties which are supposed to exist in international

[2] An attempt is made to record the more important of these in the monthly article which appears in *The Guildsman,* under the title " *Guilds at Home and Abroad.*"

trading between a Guild Socialist community and others. I see no difficulty that could not be readily overcome even in commercial relations between a Guild Socialist and a capitalist community : still less do I see difficulty in mutual trading on a basis of exchange of services between the free Societies which, I believe, will everywhere spring up on the ruins of capitalism. I do, of course, recognise that a single Guild Socialist community in a hostile world would probably have the same struggle for existence as Soviet Russia is experiencing to-day, and for that reason, among others, we must not forget that, whether or not Guild Socialism itself becomes a world-wide movement, Guildsmen are vitally interested, not only in its success, but in that of the corresponding movements, based on similar impulses and ideas, which exist in other countries. Guild Socialists, like all true Socialists, must be internationalists, and must recognise that their concern is not simply with the social system of their own country, but with the re-creation of world Society as a federation of free and internally self-governing communities, bound together by the closest ties of common civic and economic concerns, common ideas, and, perhaps above all, by that very difference and uniqueness of each which exists in the very community and without which the community would be empty and without meaning.

A NOTE ON BOOKS

There is already quite a considerable literature dealing with Guild Socialism. A list of my own books bearing on the question will be found facing the title-page. The most important books by other writers are the following:—

Hobson, S. G.	NATIONAL GUILDS, edited by A. R. Orage.
,,	GUILD PRINCIPLES IN WAR AND PEACE.
,,	NATIONAL GUILDS AND THE STATE.
Penty, A. J.	THE RESTORATION OF THE GILD SYSTEM, o.p.
,,	OLD WORLDS FOR NEW.
,,	A GUILDSMAN'S INTERPRETATION OF HISTORY.
Reckitt, M. B., and Bechhofer, C. E.	THE MEANING OF NATIONAL GUILDS.
Russell, Bertrand	ROADS TO FREEDOM.
De Maeztu, Ramiro	AUTHORITY, LIBERTY AND FUNCTION.
Tawney, R. H.	THE SICKNESS OF AN ACQUISITIVE SOCIETY.
Orage, A. R.	AN ALPHABET OF ECONOMICS.

These are all by members of the National Guilds League. So is:—

Hodges, Frank	NATIONALISATION OF THE MINES.

The only book devoted to a hostile criticism is:—

FIELD, G. C.   GUILD SOCIALISM.

But see also Bernard Shaw's essay on Guild Socialism appendix to E. R. Pease's History of the Fabian Society, and Sidney and Beatrice Webb: A Constitution for the Socialist Commonwealth of Great Britain.

There are numerous pamphlets dealing with the subject. Most of these can be obtained from the National Guilds League, 39, Cursitor St., London, E.C.4.

Of course, there are very many books which, while they do not deal directly with Guild Socialism, have a very important bearing on Guild Socialist ideas. I only set down here a very few of these:—

MORRIS, WILLIAM   SIGNS OF CHANGE.
       „   HOPES AND FEARS FOR ART.
BELLOC, HILAIRE   THE SERVILE STATE.
LENIN, N.   THE STATE AND REVOLU-
                    TION.
POSTGATE, R. W.   THE BOLSHEVIK THEORY.
LAGARDELLE, H.   LE SOCIALISME OUVRIER.
KROPOTKIN, P.   MUTUAL AID.

The list might be indefinitely prolonged into a bibliography of the classics of Socialism.

One or two more definitely specialised books should be added:—

FIGGIS, J. N.   CHURCHES IN THE MODERN
                    STATE.
MacIVER, R. M.   COMMUNITY.
LASKI, H. J.   THE PROBLEM OF SOVE-
                    REIGNTY.

The *Guildsman* is a monthly journal devoted to the propaganda of Guild Socialism. In it will be found accounts of the progress of the Guild Movement month by month. It is published by the National Guilds League.

INDEX

A

For Product Safety Concerns and Information please contact our EU
representative GPSR@taylorandfrancis.com
Taylor & Francis Verlag GmbH, Kaufingerstraße 24, 80331 München, Germany

www.ingramcontent.com/pod-product-compliance
Lightning Source LLC
Chambersburg PA
CBHW070413270326
41926CB00014B/2803